FEMINISM
V.
MANKIND

FEMINISM V. MANKIND

With foreword by Baroness Elles

FEMINISM v. MANKIND

© Family Publications, 1990

ISBN 1 871217 07 5

Published by
Family Publications
Wicken, Milton Keynes, MK19 6BU, UK
Telephone: **0908 57234**

Cover design by ***Gerald Savine***
based on the programme for the
First World Summit Meeting
"Women and the many Dimensions of Power"
Montreal, June 1990

Printed in England by
BPCC Wheatons Ltd
Marsh Barton, Exeter, EX2 8RP

Dedicated to all those men and women
who celebrate the admirable complementarity
of the sexes.

Contents

Foreword by Baroness Elles of the City of Westminster

Editor's Introduction by Christine M. Kelly

About the Authors

1. Physical and Spiritual Ecology   1
    Alice von Hildebrand

2. Feminism and the Psychologically Masculine   5
    Mary Kenny

3. Empty Hearts and Empty Homes   12
    Katarina Runske

4. Feminism and the State – the Australian Experience   19
    Babette Francis

5. The Equal Opportunities Commission   25
    Joanna Bogle

6. A Radical Feminist Charter   30
    Valerie Riches

7. Families, Feminism and Taxes   38
    Patricia Morgan

8. The Female as Hamster   46
    Robert Whelan

9. The Destructive Forces Behind Religious Feminism   53
    Cornelia Ferreira

10. The Story of Miss Teen Canada   61
    Betty Steele

Appendix: References   69

Foreword

Public opinion on social issues, formed and expressed by pressure groups through the media-press, broadcasting and publications – finds its outcome in legislation, be it national or international. The consequences therefore of public opinion, affects the lives of us all and requires a free flow of discussion and debate.

Over the last twenty or thirty years the pressure for feminist policies has been pervasive and determined, with the result that in many instances the legitimate fight for the removal of legal discrimination against women and a society offering equal opportunities based on individual free choice has been overtaken or superseded by a form of political extremism. When attempts have been made to respond to such pressures, the well-known weapon of ridicule has been used, suggesting that any woman who wished to stay at home and look after her children, for instance, is to be pitied and is of low intellectual ability. Natural instincts are to be exterminated and replaced by the search for power, an ardent feminist cause. Exploitation of the word 'equality' has been a further weapon in the hands of the feminists, disregarding the centuries-old recognition of the difference between equality and justice, spelt out in Aristotle's telling phrase, "Injustice arises when equals are treated unequally, and also when unequals are treated equally".

The lack of response to the feminists is at last being remedied. The collection of studies contained in this book by distinguished writers from many disciplines and many parts of the world is to be warmly welcomed. These writers have decided to contribute together to analyse, from their respective angles, and expose, the weaknesses and detrimental effects of feminism as portrayed by those who claim to support that philosophy. *Feminism v. Mankind* is, to my knowledge, the first serious published work which seeks to destroy the myth of feminism and to replace it with concepts of a social order based on freedom of choice, sanctity of human life and dignity of the individual, both man and woman.

At this particular time in our history, it is of the greatest significance that societies who have been living under the cold (and unsuccessful) hand of marxism are looking for an alternative way of life, democratic and free, guaranteeing human rights and restoring the role of the family, a bastion against state control.

This work will make a valuable contribution to the debunking of creeping populist theories which have held the forefront of debate for too long. It rightly seeks to restore the balance of common sense, based on practical experience, professional knowledge and innate wisdom. It should be welcomed by a wide range of readers, who, whatever their background or specific interests, are concerned with the peaceful and just development of our society.

London, May 1990 *Diana Elles*

About the Authors

Diana Elles has had a distinguished career as a lawyer and in public office and was raised to the peerage as Baroness Elles of the City of Westminster in 1972. She was Vice-President of the European Parliament from 1982-87 and Chairman of the Legal Affairs and Citizens Rights Committee of the European Parliament from 1987-89. A former member of the United Nations Sub-Commission for Prevention of Discrimination and Protection of Minorities, she is currently a member of the Sub-Committee of the House of Lords European Select Committee.

Christine Kelly has a Masters Degree in the History of Art and Design. She is a school governor in both the private and state sectors and has written and presented educational material for schools. She is married and has four children.

Dr Alice von Hildebrand is a Professor Emeritus (the first female Professor of Philosophy) at Hunter College, City University, New York and an internationally known author and lecturer. In recent years she has specialised in matters pertaining to women. Her latest book *By Love Refined, Letters to a Young Bride* addresses itself to the newly-married and has won critical acclaim in the United States and Europe.

Mary Kenny is a columnist with the *Sunday Telegraph* in London and also writes for the *Irish Independent, Daily Mail, The Tablet* and other publications in Britain, Ireland and the USA. She is an experienced broadcaster and has published four books on working mothers, Christianity and abortion. A work of fiction, *A Mood for Love*, was published in 1989; she has also written a play about North-South relations in Ireland. She is married and has two children.

Katarina Runske is a member of the Institute for Public and International Law in Sweden and President of the Swedish Family Campaign Foundation. She has lectured extensively in Europe and the Americas on human rights and family issues and contributed to many newspapers, television and radio programmes. She is married with three children.

Babette Francis was born in India but has lived in Australia since 1953. She has a BSc in microbiology and chemistry and is a trained breastfeeding counsellor. Prior to her marriage she worked in the pharmaceutical industry and as a journalist and editor. She is a founding member of *Women who want to be Women* and is its national and overseas co-ordinator. She is also a committee member of the Council for a Free Australia.

Joanna Bogle is an author, journalist and broadcaster who has also lectured extensively in the USA, Canada and Australia, Her book on traditional festivals and customs, *A Book of Feasts and Seasons* has recently gone into its second edition, and a biography of Emperor Charles of Austria/Hungary, written jointly with her husband James Bogle, is due for publication in the autumn of 1990.

Valerie Riches trained as a social worker and worked with widows and their children, then with unmarried mothers. Since becoming secretary of Family & Youth Concern in 1972 she has contributed to many national newspapers, magazines, radio and television programmes, speaking for parents and the family. She has lectured extensively in Europe, Africa, Asia, Australasia and the Americas and has written several publications on society and the family.

Patricia Morgan was Research Fellow in Socio-Legal Studies at the London School of Economics from 1979 to 1982. Her books include *Child Care: Sense and Fable, Delinquent Fantasies* and chapters in the collections *Criminal Welfare on Trial, Family Portraits, Full Circle* and *Families Matter*. She is a regular contributor to a number of academic journals and periodicals and has also written for the *Daily Telegraph*. She is currently researching her own book on the family.

Robert Whelan obtained an MA in English at Trinity College, Cambridge. He is the UK Director of the Committee on Population and the Economy and has written and spoken widely on population issues. He has written and produced a series of educational videos on social and medical issues, including *The Truth about Aids*, *The Great Population Hoax*, *Facing Facts on Population* and *The Three Rs of Family Life*. His monograph *Mounting Greenery* was published by the Institute of Economic Affairs.

Cornelia Ferreira is a writer and lecturer who lives in Toronto, Canada and is the full-time mother of four young children. She obtained a BSc in Chemistry from Marianopolis College and an MSc from Sir George Williams (Concordia) University, both in Montreal. She is the head of Women for Faith and Family, Canada, and edits its newsletter. Her other publications include *The Feminist Agenda within the Catholic Church*, *The Emerging Feminist Religion* and *RENEW: A tree rooted in Modernism and the New Age Movement*. Her articles have been published in the *Homiletic and Pastoral Review* and *Challenge*.

Betty Steele is the author of *Feminist Takeover*, a critical analysis of the women's liberation movement in Canada, which documents its radical effect on our society. Prior to marriage she was a news editor of *Marketing Magazine*, an editor of *New World Magazine*, and has written free-lance for national radio, magazines and newspapers. She has lectured throughout North America as well as appearing on television.

Editor's Introduction

A few months ago I was asked to edit a book about feminism by ten different contributors; I soon realised that I was dealing with a profoundly worrying issue. Moreover, the body of literature currently available is overwhelmingly in favour of radical feminist strategies, an imbalance which this book seeks to redress.

Australian **Babette Francis** explains the original meaning of feminism as a belief in equal rights for women, such as the right to vote, to equal pay for equal work and equal opportunities in education. Aims like these would find few opponents, and indeed an evolutionary change in the status of women in some parts of the world is long overdue. The feminism revealed by the authors is, however, not seeking an evolutionary change, but change through a revolution which would radically alter the social and economic structures of our society and especially of the family.

Canadian **Betty Steele** shows that there are many aspects of the feminist movement which are hidden to us. These go far beyond equality and are concerned rather with power and rights, grasped so militantly that other members of society suffer a kind of persecution. Men have become – on the feminist agenda – the scapegoats for the social and personal problems of women, while feminists have induced in men a sense of guilt and even hopelessness.

The book chronicles the efforts of societies everywhere trying to cope with feminism, and a picture of bewilderment emerges. Yet sense is made of this distressing situation as an international analysis, by ten contributors, deciphers the situation to reveal the reality of feminism as it alters people's lives. What emerges is a dislocation of natural order, so that men and women are no longer working for the well-being of each other, but are, rather, persuaded to aspire to life "in the fast lane", with human priorities turned upside down.

In a fascinating review of two recently published books, **Robert Whelan** discusses the researches they contain which deal firmly with the nonsense that there is no difference between men and women. **Joanna Bogle** shows how the *Equal Opportunities Commission* in Britain attempts to deny these differences, starting with the indoctrination of primary school children.

A contribution from **Katarina Runske** from Sweden tells of the trauma to children of an empty home as both parents pursue careers, forcing them into a second-place priority, cared for in creches and child-care facilities. The quest for self-fulfilment, according to feminists, must be blocked neither by child nor husband, and yet as the economist **Patricia Morgan** shows, many women have been persuaded, against their natural instincts and judgement, that fulfilment is only in the work-place. By denigrating home-making and motherhood as jobs without pay or status and by denouncing voluntary work as exploitation, feminists have caused women to forsake a worthwhile and fulfilling world, based in home and community, for the work-place and the "rat race".

Governments, anxious to recruit workers from a diminishing pool of labour have targeted women as a hitherto largely untapped resource. In this, feminist propaganda has helped them to achieve their aim. Yet, as the Swedish experience has shown, persuasion becomes coercion so that feminism, far from liberating women, is a means of denying women real choice. Thus governments allocate huge sums of money to projects which directly and indirectly jeopardise the well-being of the family. But Professor **Alice von Hildebrand** explains that strong families and good parenting make for a healthy society, whilst feminism works against this as the disturbing social statistics documented in the book show.

Feminists are eager to produce equality of effect, which is not the same as equality of opportunity, and can only be achieved by discriminating against men. One hundred countries have ratified the *United Nations Convention on the Elimination of all Forms of Discrimination Against Women*, and **Valerie Riches** points out that this means that discrimination against men and the radical ideology of feminism is enshrined in their laws. Were women to be treated in this way, it would be considered an outrage!

In the once patriarchal churches, radical feminists have already achieved power and status. **Cornelia Ferreira**, from Canada, traces the history of feminism in the churches and shows how the present situation has been reached.

Betty Steele's story of Miss Teen Canada ends the book on a note of optimism with the indication that the next generation of women may already have decided to reject the falsehoods of feminism. After all, there is no need to perpetuate the chaos and injustice of the feminist movement and indeed if, as psychologists claim, men are stunned and thus accept the feminist agenda, one day there will surely be a terrible backlash. Yet this book celebrates the greatness of being a woman and, as **Mary Kenny** explains, the power that women have always had. No doubt John Ruskin's view of women in *Sesames and Lilies* outrages feminists and yet it is a great compliment to women:

> There is not a war in the world, no, nor an injustice, but you women are answerable for it; not in that you have provoked but in that you have not hindered . . . there is no suffering, no injustice, no misery in the earth, but the guilt of it lies with you.

If it does, women must understand why and how, and that nothing can be made right and whole unless men and women work together. I hope that this book will be a resource for all those who seek justice, truth, peace and harmony for mankind.

Christine M. Kelly, May 1990

FEMINISM
V.
MANKIND

One:

Physical and Spiritual Ecology

Alice von Hildebrand

The threat of environmental devastation is very much the topic of the moment, and with good reason. Yet, if we look beyond the obvious factors of selfishness, greed and materialism, none of the proposed solutions appreciates the spiritual crisis at the heart of the ecological problem. Few seem to have noticed the profound connection between the assault on Mother Earth and the degradation of femininity and feminine values in general.

However, before one can even begin to speak about a feminine principle, one must first acknowledge that such a principle does in fact exist – sadly, something we can no longer take for granted. G.K. Chesterton's observation that we live in "a world of uncommon nonsense" might well be applied to the modern denial of the differences between the sexes. Fortunately human nature, by its very existence, bears eloquent witness to these differences, defending itself admirably against the convoluted theorising of behavioural scientists and feminists.

If we cared to observe masculinity and femininity impartially, allowing each to speak for itself, their combined message would not only provide us with a design for restoring the delicate balance between both the physical and the spiritual ecology of the world, but might very well have more far-reaching consequences for global harmony and co-operation generally.

1

How do men and women differ? Elementary observation of human physiology reveals that women are soft and flexible; men, sinewy and firm. In sexual union, woman is receptive (which ought not to be confused with passive); man is active, hence the physical impossibility of rape by a woman.

The physical characteristics have their intellectual, emotional and spiritual counterparts. A woman's psyche is predominantly affective: she is love-centred; in her, mind and heart blend admirably. Perhaps because of this, she possesses a greater capacity for self-donation and self-sacrifice. The promptings of her heart guide her mind and enable her to know intuitively that which men are more apt to deduce through reason and analysis. The French thinker, Pascal, must have had this essentially feminine trait in mind when he wrote "the heart has its reasons of which reason knows nothing".

Feminine receptivity finds its perfect expression in woman's predisposition to contemplation. Nature affords her ample opportunity to "sit in vigil on the world". One needs only to think of the quiet contemplation of a mother gazing upon the infant at her breast or the tender watchfulness of a mother over her sick child. This meditative bent accounts, too, for a woman's greater piety – women invariably outnumber men in any church congregation; her mission is "being" more than "doing". Hence she stands for universality.

By contrast men are innately directed towards creativity, activity and productivity; since they evince a remarkable capacity for separating their minds from their hearts and tend to be concerned more with ideas and objects than with persons. If a woman represents universality, then man stands for specialisation. It is no wonder that men have contributed more to art, music, architecture and invention than have women. Men have produced innumerable inanimate objects; women have given birth to human persons.

Human nature is flawed, however. A woman's rich affectivity may easily degenerate into weakness and sentimentality; her delicacy of feeling may be vitiated by a lack of objectivity. Similarly

2

a man's strength, courage and rationality may degenerate into brutality, bravado and preoccupation with objects, ideas and accomplishments.

It seems fair to say that the last centuries have witnessed a tipping of the scales in favour of the masculine principle. Our world view (in the West at least) has become increasingly object-centred, mechanistic and technologically minded. Scientific data has replaced wisdom, and activity has superseded contemplation. Our conspicuous consumption of "dreadful necessities" has lead to the destruction of the environment; and the ruthless imposition of such social and political experiments as Nazism and Communism has proved how devastating such abstract ideas can be when implemented with a callous objectivity.

Given this imbalance, one would have hoped for women to respond by advocating a return to feminine values – that would have been a proper response of common sense to "uncommon nonsense". Surprisingly, however, the women's movement has rejected the feminine traits of tenderness, humility, charity, conservation and thrift, adopting instead the masculine excesses of lust for power, success, and recognition and wanton squandering. In the process women have forfeited their chance to humanise society, and men have been deprived of the civilising influence of the female sensibility. Instead of receiving encouragement from women to direct their natural strength and single-mindedness toward noble and chivalrous ends (e.g. protecting the weak, innocent and defenceless), men have received the message – from feminists at least – that power, ambition and success are now not alone the only goods worth striving for, but are actually the ideals to which modern women aspire.

Ironically, while feminists have chosen to emulate men, many women have generally contributed to further upsetting the spiritual ecology by allowing a caricature of feminine sensitivity to permeate society. Thus we are now plagued by a nauseating "Care-Bear" culture of mawkish sentimentality, in which noble feelings have been replaced by the "warm fuzzies" and, more important, in which an entire generation of children has been lost to weak and

3

indulgent parents who confuse discipline with tyranny.

Clearly, the disturbed equilibrium in society can only be corrected by accepting, nay celebrating, authentic masculinity and femininity, their admirable complementarity and rejecting their caricatures. Moreover, neither sex can realise its own perfection without allowing the other sex to temper, shape and refine it. Without good cross-fertilisation, each sex is doomed to remain imprisoned in its own structure and fail to fulfil its mission.

If our civilisation is to survive, we must return to sanity. The masculine principle has run amok, resulting in a hyperactive pace of life, the squandering of the earth's resources and the exaltation of objects and ideas over persons. These ills will only be remedied by the healthy influence of the feminine sensibility. Only when we have learned to appreciate the art of contemplation, the "romance of thrift" (to quote G. K. Chesterton again) and the primacy of human dignity, can we begin to tackle our spiritual and environmental crisis.

Two:

Feminism and the Psychologically Masculine

Mary Kenny

When Simone de Beauvoir died, in April 1986, her reputation as the begetter of the modern feminist movement seemed secure; she, really, had written the book which started it all off, *The Second Sex*, published in France in 1949. Betty Friedan's work, *The Feminine Mystique*, published in America in 1963, merely took up the threads of de Beauvoir's thesis: Friedan's book was more accessible to the ordinary magazine reader, and was arguably more relevant to the audience it was addressing – the millions of American housewives who apparently felt suburban life to be lacking in stimulus, and were indeed manipulated by some of the cunning stratagems of consumerism. (Frieden exposed one brilliant piece of marketing that Madison Avenue had invented: after some clever man had produced a cake mix which worked perfectly well simply by adding water and shoving it into the oven, the marketing boys with psychology degrees thought it smarter to get the housewife to *beat an egg, too*, and add that to the cake mix. Then she would really get the feeling that she was "cooking"!)

Both de Beauvoir and Friedan chronicled some of the discontents of modern women; and some of these were themselves the product of social development and evolution. Many American housewives living in the suburbs of Detroit and its analogues around the United States did indeed feel a sense of isolation which, say, a woman

5

in an African village would not have felt. Technology brings its benefits; who would refuse the labour-saving advantages of the washing machine or the vacuum cleaner? But technology is *ipso facto*, isolating. Friedan shrewdly saw that the labour-saving devices – widespread in America at the beginning of the 1960s, as nowhere else – were part of the problem. The American suburban mother and wife, in the era when Friedan was writing, probably spent more time alone than any other group of women in the world. Her analysis was that women, especially if educated, wanted more meaning in their lives.

And that, she concluded, meant entering a man's world; having a full-time career; more personal freedom in the whole area of sexual politics; an escape from stereotype. Friedan's work was very much of its time, and now brings back an America which seems almost as distant as the peaceful, innocent neighbourhoods of a Norman Rockwell arcadia; yet in some respects, *The Feminine Mystique* actually spelled out the problems of affluence. If American wives and mothers were bored, as Betty Friedan claimed, it was because they had the money and the leisure to be bored. In a much more open world, now, where information technology and travel are stripping many societies bare, we can see some very different complaints from those attributed to Friedan's housewives: visit Albania, where the womenfolk work between twelve and fourteen hours a day in the fields. They do not complain of boredom, alienation or lack of personal fulfilment, but of fatigue, aching bones and lack of technology. Some discontents are the product of leisure.

With de Beauvoir, the agenda was more intense and intellectual, that of an immensely clever woman who nevertheless felt herself to be handicapped by being a woman. "One is not born, but rather becomes, a woman", she wrote in *The Second Sex*, and in that sentence lay many of the discontents of feminism today. For if one becomes a woman – rather than being born female – it follows that it is society's fault when equality between the sexes is not achieved. The shock for the little girl, says de Beauvoir, is not – pace Freud – in discovering that she does not possess a penis;

6

the shock for a little girl growing up is in discovering that she can never become like her father, in a world where men are sovereign. Thus does de Beauvoir turn around Oscar Wilde's aphorism that, alas, while all girls grow to be like their mothers, the tragedy is that no man can. In de Beauvoir's world, the shock to the feminine psyche is that all power – in the world as it is – resides in the hands of men; all authority is male; God himself is made in the image of Man.

De Beauvoir has a somewhat pathetic view of what mothers are:

The mother . . . is the one who waits, submits, complains, weeps, makes scenes: as a victim she is looked down on; as a shrew, detested . . . Her fate seems the prototype of rapid *recurrence*; life only repeats itself in her, without going anywhere; firmly set in her role as housekeeper, she puts a stop to the expansion of existence, she becomes obstacle and negation. Her daughter wishes not to be like her . . . she engages in sports and in study, she climbs trees, tears her clothes, tries to rival the boys.

Later on, de Beauvoir characterises the female again and again as passive, submissive, because society exacts this behaviour of her. Marriage has traditionally been held out to women as both protection and reinforcement of this bondage. "In marrying, woman gets some share in the world as her own; but she becomes man's vassal".

De Beauvoir is nothing if not deeply intelligent and vastly well-read; and her work is always thoughtful, as well as cuttingly honest in its assertions. Yet the trend of her thought is, if not Marxist, certainly – it seems to me – *Marxisant*, or Marx-ish; as indeed was Friedan's, in a more derivative manner. That is to say, in the thinking of these two formative writers on feminism, the idea prevails that it is *society* that always makes us what we are, rather than any natural inclination. This has flown into mainstream feminism today, and underpins the most commonplace thinking about women's roles and calling; if there are not enough women in Parliament, it is because "society" has organised it thus; if there are not enough women baggage handlers or top civil servants, it is because of flaws in society. I have grown tired of reading about exhaustive reports into the lack of top women in management, the Law or Government services. (The country which had the highest percentage of female participation in Parliament was Erich Honecker's East Germany, and a fat lot of good those conformist female communists were). Yet I, for one, do not want to take on another single responsibility. I am a mother, and, as it happens, a writer who works at home. Society should value me quite enough for being a mother; I don't need to be "at the top" in all these other worlds as well.

This negative, even wimpish view of wifehood and motherhood, both of which roles de Beauvoir refused, penetrates modern feminist thinking. Her extraordinarily weak and feeble description of a woman as wife and mother, quoted above, is in contrast to the experience of many other women who saw their own mothers as powerful characters who could make or break whole families, whole clans; matriarchs before whom the males of the domestic universe pointedly deferred. For many girls brought up in Catholic society, the most powerful – and sometimes the most terrifying – figures in their lives were nuns. De Beauvoir's world in contrast, is that of weak passive women, versus powerful, interesting men; and naturally, it follows that in such a universe any clever woman would want to be like the men.

This is the flaw that runs through so much of contemporary feminism; the notion that in order to qualify as human beings, women must somehow be more like men. Turn on the radio and you will hear the female voices on BBC's Woman's Hour pleading for women to be permitted to be coal-miners, or oil-rig workers, or, of course, priests. When the media announced that girls could be boy scouts and women could operate battleships, the news was handled as if women were being promoted because they were being admitted into a man's world!

"Progress" for women is now, above all, being represented as freedom from child-care; in order to get women into the market-place in the 1990s, it is being suggested, that both industry and

8

Government will have to provide ever more child-care, to "free" women to compete equally with men. I am not against married women and mothers of young children taking jobs if that is their choice, and they feel that they can square that choice with their responsibilities. But I am against women being dragooned into choices of any description on the grounds that a "man's world" of office, factory or plant is somehow automatically superior to a "woman's world" of home, family, and domestic sovereignty. A basic psychological problem with feminism is that they see feminine as inferior; they are neurotically bound up in their relationship with their fathers, and conceive of the whole sense of progress among women as *joining the men*. I am appalled, for example, to learn that American feminists are carrying out court cases in order to barge their way into formerly men-only clubs. The whole notion is so against personal choice and good manners. The very idea that State law should tell people that they are not permitted to run such a club is inimical to freedom and democracy. Why should feminists think that it is somehow *better* to join a man's club than to do something for themselves? The idea is in itself diminishing to women.

I am not opposed to certain aspects of feminism; to education; to financial independence; to vocational opportunity and openness within the professions, where brainpower or applied logic are required, rather than tasks of pure brawn where common sense tells us men are better adapted (and in which regard the female street-sweepers and grave-diggers of the Soviet Empire, are manifestly degraded). In February 1990, a report by a building society claimed that while the majority of women still put family life first, the majority also yearn to establish financial independence. But this is nothing new. My Irish grandmother, born in the 1870s had exactly the same idea. That a woman should always have some financial means of her own is a well-ingrained tradition in many Western cultures. Indeed the dowry was, in some societies, a symbol, not of a bride-price, but of a woman's independent financial standing, so that she should always identify her own investment in the common family property. In agricultural societies, where the division of labour followed patterns of natural biological casting, women often had their own independent means within the productive economy of the farm; in Ireland, again, the egg and milk money automatically belonged to the women. Ironically, modern farming methods, with their agri-business approach, actually withdraws such ancient entitlements from the farming woman, though farmers still enjoy the most stable of all marriages and resort to divorce less than any other group.

And as for education of women, why, the great convents were carrying out such a policy in the Middle Ages. Think of Elizabeth I, who learned Greek and Latin at the age of five; it was a well-established tradition that such women had every opportunity for education – though of course, following the culture of the time, educational opportunities were still limited by class, if not by sex.

Where I do feel that modern feminism has gone wrong is in downgrading aspects of women's lives which belonged traditionally to a woman's world; denigrating motherhood, the home and the family and relegating all vocations within the domestic arts to an inferior status. It is also wrong, to characterise the family as a merely patriarchal system which has to be thrown off (for many of the *Marx-ish* feminist thinkers, along with "Bourgeois property values"). Enormous damage has been done to the family over the past three decades, and this has hurt women, as well as children, older people and indeed men. The family is just as typically a matriarchal system, and women become strong when supported by a robust family network. Violence against women and children has increased partly, because that network of family life has been so fractured. Women have always sought to reinstate marriage whenever it has been abolished – in Russia in 1919, in Barcelona in 1936 – because for the most part marriage strengthens women's power and position, and offers protection from exploitation too. If men are more disposed to be sexually irresponsible, and promiscuous (which, statistically they are), then the bridle and yoke of marriage is civilising to some of their wilder instincts, and in the long-term interest of women.

Feminism embraces male values, when it rejects marriage, and often children (although the biological instinct to mother has overwhelmed many, even within the feminist movement). Simone de Beauvoir's own life is a rather poignant example of how preferring free love to marriage and abortion to motherhood can backlash against a woman. For most of her adult life, her partner was, of course, the philosopher Jean-Paul Sartre; she was his mistress and closest companion. In old age, as she chronicles with pitiless honesty in *Les Ceremonies des Adieux*, Sartre became querulous, senile, capricious and constantly infatuated with young women. De Beauvoir did everything that a wife would have done for him and put up with more humiliation and painful episodes than many wives might have done. When he died, she was not his legal heir, as of course a wife would have been. De Beauvoir stuck to her principles, and yet, her public position as chief bottle-washer to her lover's harem, was hardly one of personal liberation. Indeed, as a non-wife she displayed all those characteristics that she excoriated in those who "became" women: waiting, submitting, complaining, nurse-maiding an unpredictable and rather over-indulged old man, whose attention was on every passing young girl.

Women become strong – as all people become strong – by confidently being themselves; not by aping men and embracing male values. There are some straws in the wind that give me cause for confidence – it is no longer taboo, I notice, to say that you enjoy being with your children, or even that your hobby is knitting. And I'm not sure if the Green Movement isn't partly a matriarchal wave. But much of feminism is still, in effect, masculinist, and such feminism will always be psychologically confused while male envy is its base.

Three:

Empty Hearts and Empty Homes

Katarina Runske

For women in Sweden personal freedom and the pursuit of personal satisfaction represent the two most important priorities in life. This 'selfism' is taught in schools, preached by the media and promoted by women's organisations. The result is that children suffer and men despair.

Some years ago Sweden was in many respects like any other country. It was stable with one language, one predominant religion and eight million inhabitants. It had enjoyed freedom from war since 1809. In these respects it was the perfect test case to ascertain the possibility of changing the traditional structure of a nation by, to a large extent, replacing the functions of the family with the State. It is impossible to pin point when it all began in Sweden because change was not immediately apparent. It came slowly since the function of housewife and mother was, as the oldest and most important in society, the most difficult to eliminate. However it is clear that the left wing of the political system began its attack on women at home in the early part of this century. Newspapers printed stories about highly educated women who were not only accomplished at every domestic level, but who also received doctorates while they washed up and loved their husbands and children. In reality no such women existed except in the minds of propagandists, but these articles persuaded women that they had a right to a similar life-style, however unrealistic. The next step was to provide child-care which was seemingly much better than a home upbringing. Women asked themselves why they should not find a job, earn their own money and let the State look after their children. The first and perhaps most important landmark in the development of so-called women's emancipation was the publication in 1930 of the now renowned *Crisis in the Population Question*, written by the world famous Nobel prize winning couple Alva and Gunnar Myrdal. A quotation from page 249 encapsulates their opinion on housewives:

> It is still possible for weak, stupid, lazy, unambitious and otherwise lesser equipped individuals to remain and make their way within domestic work, both as housewives and as servants. As for the rest, prostitution is always available.

Mrs Myrdal became a leading authority on the emancipation of women and *Crisis in the Population Question* became the Bible for socialist women and was reprinted several times. Mrs Myrdal had three children who were looked after by nurses while she herself spent all her time working for the party. Her son, a well known author now aged sixty, has written about his childhood in several books and described his mother as an egoistic, cold woman and his father as an irritated man because he was forced to spend twenty minutes every day with his son. His books make frightening reading as they demonstrate how right the housewife and mother is and how wrong the emancipated woman is.

This man, the son of such a famous woman, had the ability and courage to put his experiences into writing. His books should be translated into every language to serve as a warning.

Mrs Myrdal and her generation established the basic pattern by which women were separated from their children, and husbands from their homes. A picture of the future for which these women worked, can be drawn from the *Socialist Family Programme* which they formulated and which is still available today. The *Programme* insisted that everyone should work, but housework was considered valueless and children viewed as obstacles which prevented a woman from earning her own living. They demanded the provision of day-care centres for all children and abortion as a right. The last sentence of the *Family Programme* reads:

Our family political programme will be the platform from which we will fight for a socialistic family politic and a socialistic society.

It showed little concern for women's wishes or the needs of children. The socialists knew that it would take some time to change the minds of women and that it was important to indoctrinate children at an early stage. They worked skilfully without taking any chances. The most important area was, of course, to change laws so that they enshrined the concept of equality in the statutes.

They achieved this quietly and without public discussion. Eventually women acquiesced in the passing of laws which incorporated the opportunity to earn money and to receive substitute care for their children. Industry needed labour and women at home were targeted as a huge potential work force. Suddenly women earned money which in turn they spent on their children in an effort to salve their consciences for leaving them alone so much. At first there were insufficient day-care centres and many children were left alone. The double-working woman was told that her life was fulfilled because she earned money. No one asked the children about their fulfilment.

Socialist policy advanced steadily and eventually a woman at home was regarded as an idiot. Succumbing to such propaganda, women were prepared to take any job in order to prove their emancipated state to their sisters. The socialist plan worked and the State provided more and more day-care centres for children. At first there were kindergartens or pre-school nurseries, but today there are day-care centres where children can be left from about six months until the age of seven when school starts. These centres are equipped with the "right" toys and the "right" food, whilst the furniture is designed for small children with even child-sized toilets. What more could a mother wish for? Doctors or other specialists are called whenever they are needed so that a mother feels confident that her child is receiving the very best care.

Indeed young mothers are persuaded that it is better care than they themselves could give their children at home. Parents do not trust themselves any longer and are afraid to take care of their own children. Mothers buy babyfood in cans in case they might cook the wrong things. Simple tasks such as boiling a potato seem to have been forgotten. When they leave hospital with a new-born baby, mothers are given papers to apply for a place at a day-care centre, together with advice about the kind of food to buy.

The cost of administering these centres is of course very high; it remains almost impossible to get an exact amount in writing from the State; but it is completely financed by taxation. When those mothers who chose to stay at home complained about the inequality of the taxation system, the State responded with the claim that working women contributed to the cost of centres through their salary deductions. In fact they used the expensive services of the day-care centres very heavily, whilst women at home used them not at all. In reality no one in Sweden pays the full cost of day-care centres where children receive all their meals, toys, books and records free. Babies are given free nappies and there is a generous child/staff ratio. Overheads such as electricity, gas, oil and water, cooking, cleaning and administration are included, so the total cost is enormous. Furthermore, day-care centre children are taken to swimming pools, theatres and concerts free of charge. The transport for such entertainment is also provided free of charge.

It proved easy to persuade housewives to work and leave their children by such inducements. Some housewives complained publicly about the inequality of their status as their emancipated sisters had gained important posts throughout Sweden. This was and continues to be yet another manifestation of the success of the socialist policy. Emancipated women speak as if for all women and thus perpetuate these policies. The opinion of dissenters is never heard.

As chairman of an organisation which has worked for the family for more than twenty five years, I have had considerable experience with emancipated women. They are supported by the Party, trained in special schools and sent on special courses. At work they enjoy free access to every modern facility. The housewife is not provided with any of these free benefits but must pay for such services as she needs them. The power of the unions which trained emancipated women increases as more women join the work force. The State provides financial aid to women who form various groups, but it has never supported the ideas of housewives.

Despite these difficulties, a society with a strong family will form and educate strong children and they will resist the impositions of the State. We who stayed at home could never have foreseen from the outset the social and political implications of the *Programme*. We just wanted the right to look after our own children and did not look upon ourselves as units within a political system. We worried about the situation for our children's sake. We saw the empty homes and read about suicides and involved ourselves in the problems that arose in schools. For us the causes were very clear: without a mother at home the family falls apart. We quickly realised the motives which were behind the family programme and saw how Sweden changed. We monitored statistics and became expert in interpreting laws which affected the family. We learned that in 1986 37,000 people married and 19,000 divorced, and that 101,950 children were born. From these figures it emerges that there were 49,300 children born to unmarried mothers. In the same year 33,100 abortions were performed.

The word family no longer exists in the Swedish legal code. It has now been replaced with words like household, which embraces the socialist view of family which might consist of two men or two women living together, with or without children. The attempted dissolution of the family has produced other problems in our society. Attendance at day-care centres apparently induced in children a state of stress. As a result teachers found it difficult to teach and children found it hard to concentrate. Teachers are leaving their profession as they are increasingly required to play a surrogate mother role. Many children in their care can neither button a coat nor use a knife and fork. These neglected children

16

pay the price of their mothers' so called emancipation.

The struggle for equality in Sweden has gone so far that today a woman can get a job simply because she is a woman and not because she is necessarily the most suitable applicant. Girls choosing a traditionally male profession receive extra points when they enter college as part of a special quota system. Similarly boys who choose typically feminine subjects receive specially favourable treatment. Such practices create a confusing world for children who are now deprived of the essential ability to recognise typical gender identities. It was not Swedish men who wanted this female revolution but rather Swedish women who were indoctrinated by the *Socialist Programme*.

The situation in Sweden is anti-family and complex:

- The law no longer protects the family.

- The housewife has no social security at all and since last year she has even been deprived of the widow's pension. Therefore every girl who wants to marry must work if only to support her family in the event of her husband's death and despite his ability to afford relevant insurance.

- The voice of women at home is not heard as women at work rationalise their life-style and together with legislation prevent the views of housewives and mothers from being publicly expressed.

- The status and joy of being a housewife and mother is joked about by so-called fellow sisters.

- Men do not protect their women any longer for they are not proud of women. Emancipated women have made it clear that they do not need men anymore, not even to become pregnant.

Most women if they understood the changes, did not want them, but were led by a vociferous few who were supported by the State. Swedish women today have been cheated into a working life and have lost their families in the process. In their old age they will

17

sit with their pensions all by themselves. Many seem to have aged prematurely trying to run double lives. But my hope for the future is the coming generation. They never liked being sent to day-care centres or the fancy toys and the high fibre food. They remember how much they longed for a day, a weekday, at home with mother. That is a very commonly expressed wish for Christmas among day-care children. Hopefully, these future mothers will not leave their children in other people's care. They would rather sell the car, move out into the country, forget about Majorca and wear old jeans in order to be able to stay at home.

A female union leader was reported in a big Swedish newspaper some years ago to be aiming for the compulsory attendance of all children at day-care centres. Her aim has been largely achieved and yet I am not so sure that the younger generation likes her ideas. The emancipated woman did not stop to consider that young people could use their brains and question their parents' life-styles. I believe in the new generation and the best thing we can do is continue our own good example and support them when they need us. Meanwhile the Socialist Party in Sweden wants to pass a law requiring every child to attend a day-care centre in order to be educated in its ideology. Such a law, if passed, will be an example of how a totalitarian State creates and consolidates through early indoctrination and manipulation of education. Let us hope that Sweden will be a warning to the rest of the world.

Four:

Feminism and the State – the Australian Experience

Babette Francis

The original meaning of "feminism" was "a belief in theory and practice of equal rights for women" and a "feminist" was an advocate for equal rights for women in spheres conventionally reserved for men. The suffragettes in Britain who agitated for the right to vote were the prototypal feminists. However, since the sixties, feminism has come to mean a specific set of methods for achieving equality between the sexes. The most significant belief underlying contemporary feminism is that there are no sex differences; therefore advocacy for equal rights must be extended to advocacy for equal results or outcomes. This article examines some of the impact this ideology has had on government policies in Australia.

Education

Through their stranglehold on the teacher unions and the education departments of Federal and State Labor governments, feminists impose their unisex ideology on the education system via "non-sexist" and "counter-sexist" programs and resource materials, most of which fly in the face of reality, denigrate motherhood and ignore scientific evidence. Euphemistic terminology such as "non-sexist guidelines" imposed on text books and curricula conceals a massive campaign of thought control and censorship to eliminate the traditional family and traditional values. "Indeed the dismantling of 'sex roles' has virtually superseded the transmission of information as the aim of the classroom".(1) "The effect of this will be to distract schools from their primary function of ensuring the best possible education for students as they attempt to meet the social and political priorities imposed by the Education Minister".(2)

Marriage and Social Security

One of the consequences of feminist antipathy to marriage has been the advent of the permissive society: alternative life-styles and no-fault divorce laws. Far from enhancing the status of women, a major consequence of no-fault divorce has been the feminisation of poverty: economic analysis indicates that after divorce, the standard of living of fathers and husbands remains the same or improves, while wives and children slip below the poverty line. Not to be daunted, feminists don't lobby for policies which will enhance the stability of marriage or even the status of wives (such as income-splitting between spouses) but lobby only for increased career opportunities for women, failing to recognise that in countries such as Australia and the USA where poverty is relative, a single mother supporting children will inevitably fall behind in economic terms compared with a couple who are devoted to each other and to the well-being of their children.

Maternity

Feminists are big on "choice" – for themselves – but not for others. They demand government-funded child-care centres so that they can seek careers while taxpayers foot the bill for the care of their children, but they object to homemaker's allowance which would give mothers, especially those in low-income groups, a real choice between caring for their children themselves or seeking careers and using the allowance to pay the cost of child-care fees. Feminists do not want mothers to have such choice because –

20

as bluntly stated by Simone de Beauvoir (author of *The Second Sex*) and Elizabeth Reid, Women's Advisor to government: "too many women would make the choice to stay at home and care for their children". Therefore fiscal, taxation and social security policies must be geared to providing incentives for women to go out to work and leave their children in child-care and should include disincentives for those choosing the vocation of homemaker. Hence the feminist obsession with getting rid of the spouse rebate which is the only financial recognition women receive for homemaking.

Employment

"Affirmative Action" is a mechanism for the preferential hiring and/or promotion of women while maintaining the pretence that employees are selected on merit. Commonwealth Employment Program (CEP) grants have been given to local councils on the basis that selection of employees is on a fifty/fifty male/female basis. This has created considerable difficulties in areas where the jobs involve manual labor, such as Jobs On Local Roads (JOLOR) projects. It is a common sight for motorists driving along JOLOR sites to observe the men doing the hard work – digging and shovelling – while the occasional female holds the STOP/GO sign: it has proved impossible to get a fifty/fifty mix as there simply aren't enough women who want to dig ditches. The worst feature of such programs is that they are presented to the public as if they were "equal opportunity" programs when they are patently aimed at "equal outcomes" regardless of the merits and abilities of job applicants. Bad enough as such obfuscation is in government projects, it is even worse when inflicted on private employers. It is obviously a dishonest feminist claim that affirmative action programs which involve targets, goals and timetables are consistent with the merit principle.

Comparable Worth

Since most feminist policies are based on intellectual fraud – the most significant being the non-admission of sex differences – their policies cannot succeed. When feminists fail to achieve their ends, they do not admit error but escalate their demands. As abortion-on-demand, permissive divorce laws, taxpayer-funded child-care centres, non-sexist education, sex-discrimination legislation and affirmative action programs have failed to produce the egalitarian unisex utopia of their fantasies, feminists simply tighten the screws. In addition to this agenda, another has been added, called "Comparable Worth", in wage fixing. It is based on the claim that women in Australia only earn 67 cents compared to every dollar earned by men because women are "locked" into a narrow range of "stereotyped" jobs which are then systematically undervalued because they are done by women. The fallacy in this circular argument is obvious - if comfortable indoor jobs which do not involve heavy lifting were paid the same as dirty outdoor manual labor, everyone would flock to receptionist' jobs and no one would want to be plumbers. The 67 cents in the dollar compares average female earnings to average male earnings, ignoring factors such as voluntary overtime, the fact that women choose jobs that combine with their homemaking role, and that they often reject promotion if it involves out-of-town transfers.

Conclusion

Feminists argue at one and the same time that there are no sex differences, but that the presence of more women in positions of power and decision making will produce a more caring society. If women are no more caring or nurturing than men, how can a society ruled by women be any different from society at present? Is Britain under Margaret Thatcher a more caring society? And if women are more caring and nurturant than men, doesn't this explain why women choose the caring vocations of mothering, homemaking, teaching and nursing, of working with people rather than machinery or abstract ideas, the so-called "stereotyped roles" which feminists so much detest? While excoriating Christian fundamentalists for their rejection of Darwinian evolution, feminists do not follow through to the logical conclusion: if the theory of evolution is valid, then natural selection must work in favour of strong, powerful men and nurturant, motherly women. A feminist is an evolutionary anachronism, a Darwinian blind alley.

In biological terms, there is nothing that identifies a maladaptive pattern so quickly as a below-replacement level of reproduction; an immediate consequence of feminism is what appears to be an irreversible decline in the birth-rate. Nations pursue feminist policies at their peril.

To do US feminists justice, many of them have publicly repudiated the ideas they once held: Betty Friedan now talks of the importance of the family. Judy Goldsmith (former president of NOW) deplores the feminisation of poverty due to easy divorce laws; and Susan Brownmiller, author of *Against our Will: Men, Women and Rape,* laments the effects of sexual liberation and the feminist adoption of the lesbian cause. "We tried to make people proud of who they were" says Brownmiller, " . . . but then the sadomasochists came out of the closet and became proud of themselves".(3) Unfortunately, Australian feminists, always a few years behind the American sisterhood, have not seen the light yet, and attempt to bulldoze through State and Federal Labor governments, policies which have a proven record of failure.

Because contemporary feminism is based on false premises, it is extremely wasteful of scarce resources. However,the most destructive aspect of feminism is that it promotes hostility between the sexes and an anti-baby, anti-child mentality among women. This is something that no community can afford − it is inimical to the survival of a society. Nevertheless, the present Labor government, while frantically searching around for cost-cutting measures in other areas of the budget, seems to regard feminist programs as sacrosanct. The Office of the Status of Women and all its off-shoots in Federal and State departments, the Human Rights and Equal Opportunities Commission, the Sex Discrimination Commission, the State Equal Opportunity Boards, the National Women's Consultative Committee and the Director of Affirmative Action could all be abolished and many would rejoice. One hopes that the federal Opposition will have the courage to operate with accurate surgery on the cancer of feminism and all its metastases which are rotting the fabric and the economic basis of our nation.

There is an important task for the Churches. If Christians believe that men and women are equal partners in marriage, then the Churches must strongly support income-splitting between spouses for tax purposes, i.e. the Churches should relentlessly pursue with the government, policies of taxation justice for single-income families, so that the homemaker's role is not merely given lip service but receives status and financial recognition.

Editor's note: This article is a slightly amended version of an original published in *Quadrant*, April 1987, and entitled "Feminism: the six frauds".

Five:

The Equal Opportunities Commission

Joanna Bogle

The **Equal Opportunities Commission** is a product of the 1970s created by the *Sex Discrimination Act of 1975*. A decade and a half after it was founded, it seems somewhat dated attempting to promote a particular set of ideas increasingly seen as anachronistic and irrelevant to women's real needs. It is perhaps the classic example of a *QUANGO – Quasi Autonomous non-Governmental Organisation* – funded by the taxpayer to the tune of just over three million pounds a year.

Many imagine that the *Commission's* main task is concerned with getting women equal pay to that of men, but this is not so. A major thrust of its activities has always been to promote specific images of women, developing a publicity and communications network which will put across a particular set of points of view.

A major difficulty for the *Commission* is its underlying assumption that "equality" between men and women can best be achieved by ensuring that all differences between the sexes are played down and by the pretence that apart from a few trifling differences of shape, males and females are essentially identical. In fact, as every development in medical science has shown us, men and women are fundamentally different in innumerable ways.

It is precisely in discovering more about these differences, and about human nature in general, that we are able to work out ways of living with one another and helping one another to resolve problems and improve our human condition.

Do You Provide Equal Educational Opportunities? is a small handbook produced by the *Commission* and reprinted at regular intervals. Under the heading "Primary Schools" it urges teachers to check on various of the children's activities:

Play activities: Are the doctors, astronauts, pirates, policemen, etc always boys? Are the nurses, hairdressers, shop assistants, teachers etc always girls? . . . Do all the parenting and family pictures used in school always show the women washing up, feeding the baby, making the beds, clearing up . . . while the man is always shown reparing the car, painting the house, reading the newspaper, going out to work, etc? Does the home corner have male and female dolls and dressing-up clothes?

The problem with this sort of approach is that it is based on presenting information which is not factually accurate. When it comes to feeding babies, it is a biological fact that women do this in a way that men can't. When it comes to pirates, history teaches us that though there were female ones, males undoubtedly predominated. The current edition of this booklet is at least better than earlier *Commission* material which listed "Red Indian Chiefs" among people who could be either male or female in children's historical games.

It is worrying to see a Government-funded publication openly advocating censorship of students' material, not on grounds of morality, good taste, or decency, but purely on the ideological grounds of feminism.

Teachers, at all levels need to select text books which present a balanced sex-role attitude, and in which not all scientists, doctors, engineers, pilots, truck-drivers, electricians etc are male and not all the shopkeepers, health visitors, nurses, play-group leaders, secretaries etc are female. Representations should be made to publishers to amend future editions of textbooks so as to present a balanced sex-role content.

It is difficult to see why the *Commission* finds it necessary to criticise boys and girls being given different tasks within a school: "Do boys always carry milk crates? Do boys and girls line up separately to move about the school?" Sometimes, members of different sexes doing different jobs can be very useful and practical, giving helpful training for the future, and a helpful imagery to the young. A major pressure on family life in Britain today is precisely that many young people growing up have poor role-models from which to learn; many come from single-parent homes or suffer a succession of broken relationships involving mother's boyfriends. A school which is a real community, in which jobs are allocated and roles worked out, as in a family, could be an excellent antidote to this and help to build up precisely those relationships and attitudes to mutual help on which a healthy society flourishes.

The *Equal Opportunities Commission* has from its inception given grants of money to groups deemed worthy of its support. These form a curiously arbitrary assortment. There are no groups supportive of traditional family life, despite the fact that it is the traditional family unit which is most under pressure today. The notion of "equal opportunities" evidently does not seem to assume an equal right to a happy marriage or secure home. There are several groups in Britain working towards such objectives – and the hope of a happy home and children is certainly one which is strong among the majority of women – but the *Commission* gives no indication of support for anything along these lines. Instead, there are grants for various industrial training schemes, to the *British Youth Council* "to produce anti-sexism training materials for use by and with BYC member organisations", and to something called *Community of Women and Men in the Church*, to "study and evaluate relationships between women and men in the Church of England".

Much more worrying, however, is the grant given to the *Brook Advisory Centres*, an organisation which specialises in giving contraceptives to boys and girls. The grant in 1988 of over £5,000 was specifically for this purpose "with particular emphasis on tackling the needs of young men". How, by any stretch of the imagination, can it be enhancing to the dignity and well-being of girls to run a campaign making it easier for young men to make use of them sexually? The suffragettes who worked so hard to try to give women their due status as citizens must be turning in their graves – and so must all those who campaigned in the last century to gain protection for young women. In the 1980s a Government-funded body turns us right back to the days of Regency bucks and the grisly early nineteenth century underworld by financing a campaign to equip young men with contraceptives in order to facilitate their sexual activities!

An Equal Start is the *Commission's* handbook for those working with pre-school children in nurseries and day-care centres. Here the chilling approach is that even warm and friendly talk must be carefully censored, lest it gives the little ones too strong a sense of their own identity and worth, when it comes to discovering which sex they are. The booklet gives examples of expressions and sentences which should be banned. These include:

Can I have two strong boys to help carry this table?
Here's a picture the girls will like. It's a wedding.
Is there a sensible girl to carry my bag for me?
Let's have a big boy to be a soldier.

It really does seem that in the *Equal Opportunities Commission's* grand scheme of things, a little girl must be trained to feel guilty if she shows too much enthusiasm for weddings. (Another section of the book warns against having "dressing- up clothes with boys and girls in mind, such as Red Indian suits for boys and bride's dresses for girls".) In this way a girl will feel guilty if she indulges too much in thoughts of weddings. So disrupted will be her understanding of her own identity that she may see her grown up role as making herself sexually available for boys who have been equipped by the *Brook Advisory Centres* with contraceptives. Is this sort of attitude really encouraging to the sense of dignity and self-worth to which every girl is entitled?

Essentially, the *Equal Opportunities Commission's* educational ideals are a series of programmes designed deliberately to blur sex

28

roles, using every possible stage of schooling to continue the message. This is surely going to create – indeed it is already creating – some very confused people, who find as they grow up that their own feelings, emotions, hopes and aspirations simply do not match up with the propaganda they are being given. It is one thing to suggest that girls should feel confident about taking on whatever their skills and talents can manage; this is helpful and challenging advice which opens up possibilities and widens horizons for them as the time for career choice arrives. It is quite another to suggest to them that it is somehow strange that they should wish to marry, raise children, and have the joy and satisfaction of running a home and developing home-making skills. It is not appropriate to suggest to them that they should repress these feelings, or that their longing for a loving husband and for babies is somehow unnatural. We are in danger of creating a new form of prudery - of being shy of things that are the most natural, satisfying and beautiful in the world.

In America, plans to introduce an *Equal Rights Amendment* into the constitution were defeated when ordinary women joined together to speak out and show what nonsense they recognised the concept of enforced unisexism to be. The *Stop ERA* campaign was run from ordinary homes and funded by the donations of individuals and organisations who had faith in the basic human qualities of men and women and believed in family life and commonsense. These campaigners took on the whole, massive federal bureaucracy and won; the *ERA* failed to get the majority it needed in the various states in the USA and it fell. It was a victory that was achieved by people simply telling the truth and stating facts about what the *ERA* would mean. Perhaps it is time that women in Britain similarly took on the *Equal Opportunities Commission.*

29

Six:

A Radical Feminist Charter

by Valerie Riches

The ponderously titled *United Nations Convention on the Elimination of all Forms of Discrimination Against Women*, was approved by the General Assembly of the United Nations and came into force in 1981. It is a radical feminist charter, which reveals the world-wide influence of radical feminist ideology. It also represents a serious threat to family life, ways of living and established legal systems.

The Convention was ratified by the British government in 1986 with minor reservations, having passed through the corridors of parliament without recourse to parliamentary debate. With its regiment of liberal feminists the media, almost to a woman, campaigned for the Convention to be ratified and any attempt to get the truth published was treated as a betrayal of women's rights. In fact it is doubtful whether the vast majority of ordinary women in the hundred countries that have ratified the Convention had any idea what was contained in this document. However, in Australia where the contents of the Convention did become known, protest was mounted and 100,000 people petitioned against it. Yet the Convention was still signed against their wishes.

The Aims of the Convention

On the cover page the Convention assures: " . . . the full and complete development of a country, the welfare of the world and the cause of peace require the maximum participation of women on equal terms with men in all fields''. We shall see that the Convention is a positive attempt to enact a crazy world view that feminists have about 'human rights' based on their opinion that there is no difference between men and women, a world in which men and women are interchangeable with every social role occupied by men and women.

It is important not to be misled by the title and to understand that to be opposed to the Convention, does not mean being for the discrimination of women. If you look at the definition of discrimination:

> any distinction, exclusion or restriction made on the basis of sex which has the *effect or purpose* of impairing or nullifying the recognition, enjoyment or exercise by women irrespective of their marital status, on a basis of equality of men and women, of human rights and fundamental freedoms in the political economic, social, cultural, civil or any other field.(1) *(author's italics)*

You will notice that discrimination is given an effects-test. Normally discrimination would be seen as a conscious act on somebody's part to treat a woman differently from a man on the basis of her sex. But here discrimination means something broader. It is any practice which has the effect of impinging on women differently than it impinges on men. This could mean that cultural practices which have grown up spontaneously without any intended malice in every field of social life, could be counted as discrimination. That is made quite explicit and it is vital to our understanding of the Convention:

> State parties shall take all appropriate measures to modify the social and cultural patterns of conduct of men and women with a view to achieving the elimination of prejudices and customary and all other practices which are based on the idea of the inferiority or the superiority of either of the sexes or on stereotyped roles for men and women.(2)

31

According to the definition, the scope of discrimination is limitless. It could be used to outlaw single sex schools, clubs, prisons, toilets and hospital wards. The phrase "irrespective of marital status" is important because none of the so-called "rights" outlined in the Convention have anything to do with marriage, including rights involving children, such as the right to adopt or to choose a family name.

The Convention claims to ensure equal rights for women, but its aims are much broader than that. It calls for "the establishment of the new international economic order",(3) for the eradication of apartheid and for nuclear disarmament. However important some may think these issues are, it is difficult to see how they relate specifically to women.

There is a significant omission. Religious rights, which are covered in all previous International Declarations on Human Rights, are not mentioned in the document.

The Convention's approach to the family is radical. It calls for "a change in the traditional role of men as well as the role of women in society and in the family".(4) We are then given details as to how all these changes are to be achieved.

Women in the Labour Force

There is an insistence, amounting to an obsession, running through the Convention to get as many women as possible to join the labour force. We are told that "Maximum participation of women on equal terms with men in all fields"(5) is necessary and that "the growth of the prosperity of society and the family" will be hampered until this is achieved.(6) Governments will be required to introduce "temporary special measures" to achieve this, and the Convention makes the point that such measures of discrimination in favour of women will not be regarded as discrimination.(7) This would appear to be a loophole to discriminate against men.

"Maximum participation of women in all fields" can only mean that the ideal envisaged by this Convention would be a workforce in which women constituted 50% of every trade and profession, however heavy and unsuitable the work.

"Temporary special measures" would mean the introduction of gender quotas and other measures of positive discrimination which are intrinsically unjust and often absurd. America has not ratified the Convention, but already has extensive anti-sexist legislation. As a result, women in New York were able to take the Fire Department to court, claiming that it discriminated against women by requiring applicants to be able to carry unconscious persons from burning buildings. The court upheld the complaint and the Fire Department was obliged to lower its standards to admit women.

Australia ratified the Convention. As a result the 1984 Sex Discrimination Act was implemented. Gender quotas were fixed for Federal Job Creation schemes, including a 50% female quota on the Jobs for Local Roads scheme. Oddly enough few women wish to build roads. As a result unemployed men were denied the right to work on the roads once the male quota had been filled.

Perhaps the most worrying aspect of the Convention's attitude towards women in the workforce is the implication that the decision to go out to work may no longer be an entirely voluntary one. Degrees of coercion may be envisaged because there is no reference anywhere to the needs of women who stay at home to look after the family – all specific health and welfare benefits called for relate to women in the labour force. To give an example, "State parties shall take appropriate measures . . . to provide special protection to women during pregnancy in types of work proved to be harmful to them".(8) If the Convention was genuinely concerned with the welfare of women, it would wish to prohibit such types of work for pregnant women, and to provide them with such support as may be necessary in the absence of a pay packet.

In Russia, the unisex Utopia envisaged by this Convention has actually been achieved, and women constitute half of the workforce. However, the status of women has not been improved. According to a leading Russian dissident and feminist, Nataly Malachovskaya, emancipation meant much harder exploitation than before. Women in the USSR are overworked, underpaid and exploited. They are forced to do hard labour and lift heavy burdens " . . . In the USSR we are all slaves, but a woman is the slave of a slave".(9)

Motherhood

Once the glory of womanhood, Motherhood is consistently downgraded in the Convention by the use of such phrases as "the function of reproduction", "the role of women in procreation", "Maternity as a social function". References to the fact that it is women, and not men, who produce babies are couched in negative terms, as if to ensure that women get back to work as soon as possible after childbirth. Jobs must be kept open and governments will be obliged to provide "a network of childcare facilities".(10) Apart from the cost to the taxpayer, the effect on family life of such policies would be seriously disruptive. The needs of women who do not want to join the labour force, or may not wish to return to work after the birth of children are completely ignored. Whatever does the Convention mean when it calls for "a proper understanding of maternity as a social function"? Are children born to parents or are they the property of the State?

Mind Control

Perhaps most destructive of all the measures in the Convention is the call "to modify the social and cultural patterns of conduct of men and women".(11) Here we enter into the area of mind control. Governments will be obliged to alter their people's cultural patterns in order to conform to standards dreamt up by a committee of 'experts' at the United Nations.

The Japanese philosopher Michito Hasegawa has accused the Convention of cultural colonialism. She has written:

The cultures of individual nations and ethnic groups merit mutual respect, not arbitrary modification by outside forces . . . So much suffering has been inflicted upon the people of the world by the white race's belief that its culture alone is universal, with

34

the consequent imposition of its religion, languages, customs and values on other cultures . . . An attitude that casually calls for modification of cultural patterns without consideration of differing cultural systems is the epitome of colonialism.(12)

In order to achieve the modification required by the Convention there must be "the elimination of any stereotyped concept of the roles of men and women at all levels and in all forms of education . . . in particular, by the revision of textbooks and school programmes and the adaptation of teaching methods".(13)

What this means is a systematic censorship of textbooks and the supervision of children's behaviour with an eye to convince them that there is no difference between boys and girls. This is brainwashing quite literally. Children are to be convinced that their perception of the obvious physical and psychological differences between the sexes has always been wrong. A family situation where mother stays at home to look after the children would be classified as stereotyping. So our children would be propagandised by those who wish to effect a change in the pattern of family life.

There is already ample evidence of the way in which groups and individuals who are opposed to the family have used anti-sexist education. Church schools in London were under pressure from the Inner London Education Authority to eliminate material promoting marriage and the two parent family as the context for raising children. In Tasmania the local education authority sent a team of anti-sexist librarians into a school to purge its library of over five hundred 'sexist' books, including *Snow White, Born Free* and *The Bible*.

Enforcement

The Convention was specifically designed to be legally binding on ratifying governments which are then obliged to submit regular reports to a Committee of Experts. If the committee complains about lack of progress towards United Nations' ideals and these cannot be settled by arbitration, the issue can be taken to the International Court of Justice. The original Committee of "twenty-three experts of high moral standing and competence"(14) contained representatives of fourteen nations listed by Amnesty International for the use of torture, including Vietnam, the Philippines, the Soviet Union and China.

In this respect, the Convention refers to the "same rights to decide freely and responsibly on the number and spacing of children".(15) Fine. But China has ratified the Convention and China mandated abortion for women who already have one child. How could China ratify a document which gives the right to freely decide on the number and spacing of children and also practice compulsory abortion? Look at the wording again. It does confer the right to decide freely on the number of children – freely and *responsibly*. Thus the Chinese government can say "We have a population problem. Women who want more than one child are behaving *irresponsibly* and have therefore foregone their right to decide on the number of children". In China, apparently you can decide freely, but you cannot decide freely and *irresponsibly*.

The International Planned Parenthood Federation has already revealed in a report(16) that it intends to use the Convention to implement its policies:

> The right to family planning, although a newcomer to the catalogue for human rights, can be legally enforceable by attaching it to one or two of the most basic human rights . . .
> The human right to family planning is included as a element of non-discriminatory rights in the *Convention on the Elimination of All Forms of Discrimination Against Women*. This *Convention* is legally enforceable.

Under the terms of this report 'family planning' means contraception, abortion and sterilisation for all, including children from the age of ten, without parental knowledge or consent.

With the force behind it of its legally binding status the Convention is a powerful means by which to spread the vagaries of extreme feminism. Our life-styles, family lives, working lives and our freedoms are in jeopardy. As a leading feminist, Gloria Steinam, has said: "We have to abolish and reform the institution of marriage . . . by the year 2000 we will, I hope, raise our children to believe in human potential, not God''. She also said: "We must understand what we are attempting is a revolution, NOT a public relations movement . . . it is humanism that is the goal''.(17)

The United Nations Convention on the Elimination of all forms of Discrimination Against Women has given the feminists the tools to achieve their world-wide humanist revolution. You have been warned!

Seven:

Families, Feminism and Taxes

Patricia Morgan

The power game

A couple may think that they are distributing their labour to maximise their mutual advantage if one specialises in child rearing and household management, while the other provides the material means of support. It is a complementary relationship of exchange, where the family expresses the way in which human life is a system of mutual obligations and dependences.(1) If people who live together choose freely that one will earn money, while the other works for the general good in another way, what is exploitative or unjust or despicable about that?

Feminists disagree. For them the family is the "key institution for the determination and perpetuation of women's subordination"; the place where oppression is most "excruciatingly experienced".(2) Marriage, with "its legal obligations, institutionalised male authority and compulsory heterosexuality" is "incompatible with sexual freedom". The domestic division of labour is a shadow play of a power struggle between oppressor and oppressed, where the husband enslaves the wife through her dependence on his wage earning on the one hand and by blocking "access to material resources outside the household" on the other.(3)

Using this analysis in *Inside the Family*, Melanie Henwood for the Family Policy Centre (funded by the UK Government), sees the extent of domestic specialisation or complementary arrangements as indicative of the pervasiveness of the 'war between the sexes'. The ways in which families organise domestic tasks, child rearing and paid work are nothing but aspects of the distribution of 'power'(4) insofar as any division of labour pertains, so "power has not been distributed equally in more than a few families". That couples believe their arrangements are 'natural, right and best' and justify them by reference to the demands of parenthood only produces consternation at their apparent satisfaction with these "inegalitarian arrangements".

But, if the division of labour is war, its opposite is 'symmetry' where husbands and wives have identical roles; do identical amounts of paid work as well as an identical percentage of the same household chores and child-care tasks, go to an identical number of business conferences and even have identical periods of leave after a birth.(5) This is 'true egalitarianism', because only here can the spouses 'confront' each other with equal 'power'. Thus, contrary to what most people would understand

> . . . a greater equality of status and a greater sharing of other aspects of life, (such as mutual interests and leisure activities within the modern 'companionate marriage') *need* not indicate domestic equality.(6)

Never mind that 'symmetry' negates the possible gains of marriage; replaces the exchange relationship with occupational competition and vastly increases the total workload. Instead of spouses collaborating to put breadwinning and homemaking in the service of parenthood, the goal of individual career advancement is primary. Men and women run on parallel lines: "two equal wills, and no mediating principle to link them . . . "(7)

The barriers to equal outcome

Clearly, the aim of the 'equal rights' movement for "equal representation of men and women at all levels in each trade and profession" (a Liberal and Social Democratic Alliance policy proposal of 1986) is also the vital means to smash men's domination at home.(8) "Marriage", family sociologist C.C. Harris informs us, "will be perceived as oppressive . . as long as they (wives) cannot, for whatever reason, participate on equal terms with men in the labour market".(9) And here, two fat volumes for the European Commission explain how women's anticipation of parenthood and the fact that it is "mothers who bear the brunt of basic child care tasks" makes it "harder for women to gain access to internal labour markets or to progress within them"; placing them "at a great disadvantage in competing with men . . ."(10)(11) So, the "worlds of employment and the home then form a complex and pervasive dialectic", where

A vicious circle operates: lack of power within the market place reinforces powerlessness within the home and in the political arena which, in turn, feeds back into the labour market.(12)

Yet, single women's earnings are very close to single men's and the remaining gap owes much to the number of single mothers on welfare. Obviously, it is the proportion of women out of the labour force or working part-time *at any one time*, which results in the failure to achieve the perfect statistical equivalence in pay and position desired by those who want complete equality of outcome. In fact, child rearing makes little difference to women's overall labour market participation and achievement *over time*.

But, as women have less children, return to work sooner after birth, and are more likely to work between births, this only seems to pin-point how "having children disrupts women's employment"; highlighting the fact that children are the single greatest 'obstacle' to equality.(13)(14) Parenthood means

. . . a net loss of over six years of paid work . . . a typical woman in the UK having two children in her late twenties has nine years less full-time employment, but 2.8 years part-time employment . . . (15)

In comparison, "men pay no such price for parenthood".(16)

Malevolent breadwinners?

No price? The bulk of income supporting families comes from men's earnings, which they might otherwise spend on themselves. Who precisely is being sacrificed to whom when British fathers work the longest hours in Europe (a third putting in more than 50 hours a week), with many taking second and even third jobs as they try and counter the economic liabilities which have piled up against families.

But this cuts no ice with those who see only moves to consolidate domestic domination which, strange to say, does not pay for anything. The doctrine is that a woman is poorer than her husband to the degree that she earns or otherwise receives less than he does, with non-earning wives and children destitute – if it were not for the £7.25 per week *Child Benefit*. In addition, it is not just that husbands do not hand over, or pay for, much – if anything, it is also because, appearances not withstanding, economic dependency equals 'hidden poverty' which exists insofar as even the wife of a millionaire is 'unwaged' and does not receive an "independent income" from the state or the market. Thus, "caring is what they do and poverty describes the circumstances in which they do it".(17)

Meanwhile, the husband is somehow building himself a lush life in a different dimension from that occupied by his indigent wife and children; his life "largely unaffected by fatherhood . . . enhanced by marriage".(18) Pre-occupied with self-aggrandisement, fathers are 'irresponsible', 'uninvolved' when it comes to child-care and "everywhere put their interests before those of women".(19) With nothing for families in these worthless, even malign, activities of father, the reports to the European Commission complain how nevertheless,

> In many marriages, wives are still expected to provide, and often do provide, support services to their husbands, which benefit them in various ways, including their employment. Some of these services are practical – cooking, washing and ironing clothes; others are emotional – providing encouragement, showing sympathy and support.(20)

Central to all proposals to change this state of affairs through financial incentives as well as re-education is the elimination of the man's breadwinner role and breakdown of "the expectation that women will be responsible for caring".(21)

What people want for Families

Yet, over three-quarters of both husbands and wives define male parenting to include being a good provider. Over 90% of mothers insist that their family is more important than other domains of life. A majority of non-employed women give looking after children as their main reason for being economically inactive, and they do not consider themselves unemployed.(22) Only 20% of the respondents to the *British Social Attitudes Survey,* wanted to see the mother of a pre-school child go out to work at all (with 3% supporting full-time).(23) The 'traditional' only gives way to a 'compromise' arrangement for households with children in their teens so that, by a margin of four to one, people prefer women with teenage children to work part-time. Women no more favour the mothers of small children working than do men.

There is a gulf between what people would like to happen and what they actually do. As many as 70% of those from households with full-time working wives believe that mothers of young children should stay at home and only a quarter opt for the 'equality' solution for families with teenagers.(24) Family and child rearing are central and overriding values in their own right, and any withdrawal of women from the labour market when child rearing demands are heaviest, reflects a preferred solution rather than an imposed one. Yet, those who make much of financial dependence in the family as the graveyard of female freedom are not averse to using the power of the state to control the choices of every woman. This subordination of the wishes of women to the ends of others is justified on the grounds that women are 'forced out of work' and 'trapped at home' against their will or do not know their own minds, i.e. they are worms or imbeciles.

Planning for other women

The plan for women invariably involves the support of children devolving upon the 'self-sufficient' mother. But, so that they do not 'blight' her chances and get in the way of her free development, communal care is necessary from early babyhood and custodial provisions for older children out of school hours. So, there must be publicly provided free or low cost day-care centres; vouchers or child-care allowances which could be redeemed by minders or care programmes, or tax relief for child-care – or a mixture of all three. Since help is only for children who go into third party care, parents who raise their children at home will subsidise families where both parents are in full-time work, while receiving no relief themselves.

At the same time, it is often insisted that there are "certain types of 'families' " which *positively* need "defending – single parents and their children, gay couples and lesbian mothers".(25) But, these are "under attack because they do not conform to the family ideal", when 'splitting up' and single parenthood is a liberating experience and a means of "breaking free", not only for the women who resent "the freedom they lost, the restraints of children and domesticity" but "also for the children involved".(26) Catherine Itzin muses on how "single parent familyness *(sic)* as a properly serviced status" might become "quite as desirable an option as marriage – perhaps more so for some people."(27) Made more economically attractive "single parent families . . . would threaten the existing social structure." Fran Bennett of the Child Poverty Action Group concurs: "an income as of right for women – and lone parents in particular . . . might tempt them (mothers) out of the nuclear family set up". (Of course, the present UK tax benefit system hardly favours married parents, heterosexuals or non-working parents – very much the reverse.) But what of men? They have got to be continually 'confronted' and 'pushed' to discard notions of personally supporting and protecting any offspring they might spawn and "take responsibility for children and all those in need of care and support" by paying for the creches and welfare mothers.(28)

This exemplifies the differences between *family policy* or *family equity* and what feminists see as *sexual equity*. The one endeavours to ensure parity in living standards between those with and without the charge of children through compensatory measures, including tax reliefs, family allowances, housing assistance and help in kind. These are aimed at ensuring the cohesion, integrity and viability of the family unit; helping its members contribute to the welfare of the whole. In contrast, the other hopes to use fiscal and other measures to

> ... undermine the different family responsibilities of both sexes; the women might no longer feel dependent on the men, and the men might no longer want to provide for their wives and children.(29)

We are all self-sufficient working mothers now

There is easy movement between the notion that the one-earner family should not exist, to the belief that it does not. So at one moment marriage (or transferable) allowances are undesirable incentives to keep mothers at home and, at the next, ". . . totally unsuited to the twentieth century, when most working families are dependent upon two incomes".(30) Part-time work is read as full-time work and that women work at some periods in their life means that they work at all times. The "non-working wife, now very much in the minority" soon becomes the atypical non-working mother.(31) More *women* are said to be in full-time work than devoted to full-time child-care so, ergo – more *mothers* are devoted to full-time work than full-time child-care.

The next step is to make all employed women become entirely self-supporting: "so many married women are not in fact dependent upon their husbands for income". This then proves that male provision for families is already extinct because " . . . most married women work outside the home".(32) The household not fully dependent upon the husband's income at *some times* is seen as independent of it *at all times*. Where a woman's earnings brings the family income over the poverty line, she is then assumed to be the only support. Never mind that two-thirds of women with a child under five stay at home full time, and 25% have a part-time job (often under ten hours a week). By the time all children are at school 60% of mothers have gone back to work, but only 16% full-time. With the youngest child ten, 30% are still at home and 45% in part-time work, while those in 'full-time' jobs usually get home by 5 p.m.

Have families no alternative to double income and creche?

It is said that mothers *must* work – a singularly graceless argument coming from those who want to force all women to work, and are prepared to further impoverish families to do it. (The same goes for arguments from demographic inevitability). Certainly by the 1970s, families required two wage earners to achieve the same standard of living they could have achieved with one in the 1950s. But, that many mothers work from necessity is a reason for regret, not a cause for celebration. Blaming the one-earner family because it is here that poverty and hardship is concentrated, conveniently ignores the way in which government economic management no longer proceeds with an eye on the 'family budget' and its impact on the interests of families.

But, incongruously, if families are to 'afford' the solution to the poverty of double earners, they must be provided with free or heavily subsidised day-care. It might be less expensive, cumbersome and acceptable to provide parents with assistance to raise their own children in the first place by increasing disposable income. A way to both reduce economic constraints on families and give them real choice, lies through a return to the considerations they once received; then, if families want to use relief to care for their own children they are free to do so, as others are to purchase services outside the home. People who look after each other and their own children deserve at least equal treatment and should not be cast apart.

Eight:

The Feminist as Hamster

Two Book Reviews by Robert Whelan

The Great Sex Divide: A Study of Male-Female Differences
by Glenn Wilson, Peter Owen, £14.50

Brain Sex, *by Anne Moir & David Jessel, Michael Joseph, £12.95*

In *My Fair Lady,* the musical version of Bernard Shaw's *Pygmalion,* the exasperated Professor Higgins sings *Why can't a woman be more like a man?* This is a question which feminists have been posing for some time now, and the answer they come up with is briefly this. Women are not like men because they are moulded by society into an inferior role, consigned to the status of second class citizens, allocated the most uninteresting and lowly paid jobs and treated as breeding machines to produce the next generation.

The answer, as feminists see things, is simple. We must change the structures of society to give women a fair chance. Education must encourage girls to take traditionally male subjects, like engineering, and to see their future in terms of high-level job achievement, not of motherhood and the home. Equal opportunities legislation must force employers to take on female quotas, even if it means accepting women who are less qualified than competing men, as a means of righting the wrongs of past generations; and men must be made to take on a more domestic role in running the house and looking after the children so that women can achieve these new goals.

This feminist blueprint for society is based on a fundamental assumption about sex roles, which is that they are interchangeable. Men and women are seen as being basically the same sort of animal. Differences in aims and achievements only reflect society's 'conditioning'. It should therefore be possible to change men and women by changing the conditioning process.

As a result of a great deal of research which has been conducted in the last ten years, we now know intellectually what common sense has always told us instinctively: this is not true. These two books both draw on much the same research, and even tell some of the same stories to show that men and women are fundamentally different. Furthermore this difference is more profound even than the fact that men have penises and women have wombs. It is a difference which begins with the brain and the weight of scientific evidence on this question of differences in the male and female brain is now overwhelming. Put briefly, the different functions of the brain are shared between the right and left hemispheres, but they are for the most part more precisely located in the male brain, and more diffuse in the female. It is for this reason that, when brain damage occurs, the vital question in the case of a woman is the extent, and in the case of a man, the location of the damage. The female brain may be able to make up for damaged areas by 'supplying' functions from another part of the brain, where a man would lose functions entirely.

The two hemispheres of the brain are linked by a set of neural 'jump leads' called the corpus callosum. These 'leads' are thicker and more frequent in the female brain, which means that more information is exchanged between the different parts of the brain. This may be the explanation for the legendary 'female intuition'. Women can connect verbal and emotional information faster than men. A woman can 'sense' that her husband is lying to her, or that two close friends are having an affair, because she can connect what she is hearing with emotional data like bodily attitudes and the degree of eye contact. A man would hear the information he was being given, but would miss out on the emotional sub-text.

Because male brains have their functions more clearly separated, this may explain the greater determination and ability to succeed in any given field. It seems that men can concentrate single mindedly on a particular objective, whilst a woman would be more distracted by other – important – considerations. Thus a man can pursue career goals relentlessly, to the destruction of his health and even his family life, when a woman would be more circumspect.

In addition to this, the concentration of visuo-spatial perception in the right hemisphere of the male brain makes men more capable of handling spatial concepts like abstract, intellectual thought. This is why men excel at maths, astronomy, musical composition, physics and most scientific pursuits. Women, on the other hand, have their verbal skills more concentrated in the left hemisphere. They learn to handle language faster than boys, and the fields in which women excel like literature (e.g. Jane Austen, Virginia Woolf) are those which depend on verbal skills, emotional perceptiveness and human sympathies.

In a passage which has probably put him high on the feminists' hit-list, Glenn Wilson has this to say about genius in *The Great Sex Divide*:

> Virtually all of the people throughout history whose achievements are acknowledged as products of undisputed genius have one thing in common . . . they are all male.

He attributed this to the more specialised functions of the male brain which allows for greater concentration on a given object; on the aggressive and competitive instincts which are produced by male hormones; and on the lack of respect for rules and formulas which drives a man to find out whether the sun is really going around the earth as the priests once said, or not.

To the feminist, or environmentalist argument that different levels of achievement reflect society's preconditioning or prejudice, Wilson replies that societal preconceptions have little or no influence. He cites the specific case of musical composition:

> For hundreds of years European ladies have been expected to sing and play an instrument such as the piano as a social grace

and yet the greatest composers have without exception been men.

Moir and Jessel agree that occupational roles are determined by brain structures:

Boys and men live in a world of things and space, girls and women in a world of people and relationships.

However, neither of these books subscribes to the view that 'women's work' is less important than men's. It is indeed the feminists, who are determined that women must prove themselves through success in scientific achievement or the company board room, who down-grade traditional female roles, making wives and mothers feel guilty and unfulfilled. Women need not view their work as inferior, unless they take on the male mindset and insist on viewing the world through men's eyes.

According to both books brain differences resulting from chemical changes in the womb account for the differing attitudes shown by men and women towards sex. In fact, there is probably no area in which the feminist claim that men and women are the same, except for the opportunities given to them by society, is more patently absurd. Men are by instinct dominant, questing, promiscuous and glad to have 'sex for sex's sake'. Women are more interested in relationships, home-making and establishing a secure 'nest' for the rearing of offsprings. They are consequently more reticent in the granting of sexual favours, and less interested in 'recreational sex'.

For more than twenty years now we have been bombarded by feminist concepts of the 'new man' and the 'new woman'. The new woman is supposed to be raunchy, independent, ambitious and self-sufficient. The new man is supposed to be gentle, caring and submissive. Both are chimeras which have sprung from the minds of social engineers.

Wilson observes that whatever the feminists and social engineers might claim or demand, the male is the dominant species, not only in humans but throughout the animal kingdom, with the peculiar exception of the hamster. This struck a personal note with me as I used to have two hamsters, a male and a female, when I was a child. I will never forget the day when I went to the cage to find that the female had disembowelled the male and torn him limb from limb. Is this the fate which lies in store for increasing numbers of males in Western societies, as they succumb to a feminist agenda? We must hope not.

Both books quote a considerable body of evidence that social engineering will never overcome biological programming. Perhaps the most significant was the failure of the Israeli kibbutz to break down normal family relationships.

When the kibbutz were established in Palestine in the early part of this century there was a deliberate intention to abolish sex differences by relieving women of the 'burden' of child-care. Marriage was replaced by co-habitation. Children were reared in communal nurseries, where they ate, played and slept. Particular contact between parents and children was discouraged. All educational and recreational arrangements were unisex. Feminine clothes, hair-styles and make-up were rejected. Women were encouraged to play an active part in kibbutz government, as well as in all manual labour and economic activity.

When anthropologists Melford and Audrey Spiro visited the kibbutz in 1950 they thought the unisex dream had come true. All sex differences were thought to have been shown to be the result of social programming.

However, when Melford Spiro returned in 1975 he found striking changes which "all but undid the earlier revolution".(1) Marriage had returned with full ceremonies. Parents were demanding access to their own children, who now slept with them and not in the dormitories. Government of the kibbutz had become predominantly male, and men did most of the economically productive work, while women had reverted to traditionally female roles in teaching, nursing and housework. Women had also returned to traditionally feminine styles of dress, of behaviour and pastimes. As the *New York Times* (April 1976) observed:

In the one place where feminists thought their ideal existed, the feminine mystique is ripening as fast as the corn fields.

This is not to say that feminism is harmless. It continues to blight the lives of many, particularly those women who are convinced that they are failures unless they succeed on the same terms as men.

The sort of 'sexual fascism' (to use Moir and Jessel's term) which is necessary to change human beings to fit a new ideology is now evident at every level of society. It is easy to laugh at its more absurd manifestations, like the word-processing package which inserts "or she" every time the operator types "he"'. Less amusing are the socially engineered, anti-sexist courses of propaganda used in schools. They begin with non-sexist fairy stories about princesses fighting dragons to save princes, and end with bigoted teachers pushing girls into courses of study for which they may have no aptitude, in order to maintain the sort of quotas which are beloved of the educational establishment.

Wilson ends his book with a telling quote from, of all people, Joanna Foster of the Equal Opportunities Commission:

American women climbed up the career ladder fast; but when they got to the board room they looked around and saw that all the men had pictures of their families on their desks. The women didn't have any pictures of their families. They didn't have any families.

And what of the most numerous class of victims of feminism – the women who stay at home to be housewives and mothers and find themselves branded as low-achievers, or even traitors to their sex, as a result? According to Moir and Jessel:

Being a parent is no push-over for a mother, but at least she comes with all the right equipment – perceptual, cognitive, emotional as much as anatomical. And, whatever the new liberationists teach her, she usually wants to be a mother. Yet just at the moment when women are freest to enjoy and exploit their natural, superior skills of motherhood, a stern sisterhood

51

tells them that this is an unnecessary, low-value and socially regressive role.

We must hope that the absurdity of feminism will eventually lead to its collapse. We will then be able to confine its claims to the realm of mythology where it will join those romantic tales of fierce tribes of Amazonian women who led their people into battle. Of course the warlike Amazonian women never existed. Neither do the interchangeable men and women of the feminist Utopia.

Nine:

The Destructive Forces behind Religious Feminism

Cornelia R Ferreira

Feminism is a tree with two branches: secular feminism, found in society; and religious, spiritual or Christian feminism, found in the Church. Both branches have the same roots (their common beginnings) and trunk (their similar goals and philosophy). So the history of religious feminism is inextricably bound up with that of secular feminism, and cannot be studied apart from it. Although this article chronicles the evolution of North American feminism, it pertains equally well to European feminism, which has developed in the same way. In fact, feminism's philosophical base and momentum hail from Europe, as will be seen.

Feminism, as a political force, came into being in the nineteenth century as the suffragette movement, whose original goals for civic reform were legitimate. Then, at the turn of the century, the two ideological branches developed that brought feminism into direct conflict with Christianity and Christian civilisation: the secular, which adopted Socialism, and the religious, which sought a return to pagan spirituality. However, Socialism prevailed in both branches and it was not until the 1970s that mainstream religious feminism adopted paganism as its spirituality.

Both ideologies stemmed from a "quest for the lost past" to find historical precedents for women's equality with men and it is in this quest that we see the feminist tree rooted squarely in the fertile soil of *imagination*. Arch-religious feminist Rosemary Ruether freely admits that this quest involved "speculation" adapted from Germanic "romantic" anthropological theories that imagined "matriarchy as a universal state of civilisation before patriarchy".(1) Victorian feminists, all "post-Christians",(2) then "imagined alternative religious and social systems for the future" based on the fantasised values and social orders of "prepatriarchal matriarchy" which they considered superior to Christianity and the Judeo-Christian social order.(3)

Feminist socialism envisaged primitive matriarchal society as a "communal egalitarian society" where "woman existed as a free person whose labor and sexuality was at her own disposal". Patriarchy, emerging "through the rise of private property", ended "matriarchal communism", bringing about "patriarchal individualism" and "the subjugation of woman". Feminist socialists desired an "egalitarian society which will reclaim women's rights, while at the same time appropriating for women the individualism won by males under fraternal patriarchy".(4)

But feminist socialist ideology arose only *indirectly* from "romantic" anthropology. The theory of primitive matriarchy, first broached by *men* to show that its supercession by patriarchy was inevitable and an expression of progress,(5) obviously suited Communist goals, because it was "absorbed into socialism" by Engels.(6) *It was from Communist theories that feminist socialism emerged* "as part of a comprehensive view of social progress" that desired to "better" society and religion by supplanting the Western social order and Judeo-Christian religions with the values of earlier cultures.(7) Based on these illusory, romanticised values, feminists "sought to render Western biblical and social history non-normative, a passing phase of a larger scheme of social development that looked back to earlier origins".(2)

Going one step further back, we see the hand of Freemasonry in the evolution of feminism. Cardinal Caro y Rodriguez of Chile documented the following sentiments of an Illuminati chief: "Women have a very strong influence over man, so we can reform the world if we reform women".(8) Mixed lodges were established

54

to train women to shed their modesty and delicacy and to teach them hatred toward Catholicism.(9) Furthermore, Communism itself is a Masonic instrument. Marx and Engels were commissioned by the Illuminati to write the *Communist Manifesto*, whose ideas reflected Illuminati thinking.(10) Marx wanted to abolish the family and make women the property of the state,(10) whilst Engels, as seen, lured women into accepting the Masonic/Marxist design for women.

Two different ideologies also characterised nineteenth-century *religious* feminism. The first, involving only a small minority, was a "quest for the lost past" to find "a larger wisdom that would be at once more universal and more immanent to one's psyche and bodily processes than that provided by Christianity". These women looked to ancient cultures for a "wisdom" that had suffered a "lamentable conquest by Christianity and patriarchy".(2) Matriarchal society with its idea of female divinity and the worship of the Mother Goddess was touted as "the golden age of human society that was over thrown by the regressive influence of . . . patriarchal religion" which "displaced an earlier era of women's power".(11) These "spiritual" feminists "sought to revive the ancient matriarchal culture and religion, with its female symbols of the divine, as the more appropriate vehicle for female empowerment".(12)

Matilda Joslyn Gage was "convinced that the Christian Church was the prime source of the oppression of women"(13) and Elizabeth Cady Stanton stated, "The emancipation of women is . . . impossible, unless the Bible is understood from a feminist perspective and repudiated as revelation".(14) She, Gage and others produced *The Woman's Bible*(13) but this attempt to revise Scripture was ahead of its time and "faded into oblivion, to be rediscovered" in the 1960s.(14) The "return to the Goddess" movement suffered the same fate until the 1970s.(12)

The second ideology that developed in early religious feminism was socialism, which was brought into the Church by Christian suffragists. Socialism became firmly intertwined with their religious beliefs and in 1897 Christian suffragist Frances Willard probably expressed the majority view when she "declared that 'true Christianity is socialism and true socialism is Christianity'".(15)

Christian socialists considered the all-male priesthood a repudiation of their understanding of "equality" for which they obtained Scriptural justification by misconstruing *Galations 3:28*, "There does not exist among you Jew or Greek, slave or freeman, male or female. All of you are one in Christ Jesus". Rejecting the Christian teaching that this statement refers to the spiritual equality of those who live in faith,(16) feminists perceived this equality as having existence only on a human plane. So they started demanding an "institutional reform that included women in the . . . ordained ministry".(17)

The issue of women's ordination, thus having a spurious Scriptural justification, became a civil rights issue around which the Christian feminist movement coalesced. According to Ruether, as "the ideals of 'neither male nor female' of the New Testament ceased to be seen as beyond nature and became a goal of social reform", "eschatology was . . . brought down from heaven and located in the future, as the goal of a historical process of . . . amelioration of unjust social conditions".(17)

Feminism subsided noticeably between the two World Wars, perhaps because the suffragettes had attained their goals.(18) Further, the theory of matriarchy as a universal state of civilisation before patriarchy was discredited by anthropology and by the reaction against Victorianism. With its emphasis on the superior moral values of a womanhood rooted in maternity, "Victorian culture no longer attracted the post-suffrage generation". At the same time, the pictures "of superior moral womanhood found in theories of ancient matriarchy" were viewed as *backward projections of Victorian values* and so these theories fell into disfavour in the general reaction against Victorianism.(19)

However, classical archaeology, classical mythology and schools of Jungian psychology whose interpretations of ancient myths even Ruether questions, wondering whether they are actually "projections of a European romantic culture", preserved the idea of ancient matriarchy.(20) Also during this period, the secular humanist and occult arms of what would later be called the *New Age Movement* were quietly being developed; these would greatly influence feminism's second wave.

This wave, which surged up in the 1950s, was a full-fledged revolt against womanhood itself. Very evident in the new feminists was the loss of modesty, delicacy and the nurturing qualities of womanhood – a triumph of Masonry? Simone de Beauvoir heralded the resurgence of feminism in *The Second Sex*. This 1949 book was outspokenly Marxist, but because Marxism was not publicly acceptable, it did not sell well at that time.(21) Nevertheless, it later became the "bible" of modern feminism and of so-called "feminist theology".(22)

But it was psychologist and secular humanist Betty Friedan who provided the impetus for feminism's second wave. The thesis of her 1963 consciousness-raising book, *The Feminine Mystique*, was that women had been *brainwashed* into seeing the "sexual roles" of wife and mother as the only desirable goals for them. Friedan made "housewife" a derogatory term for the full-time wife and mother. Her thinking was influenced by Abraham Maslow,(23) an early leader of the human potentiality movement (a branch of Secular Humanism), which sees individuals evolving into gods and independent of the authority of governments or traditional religion. Friedan advocated "a drastic reshaping of the cultural image of femininity", because women's existing culture did not permit them to "gratify their basic need to grow and fulfil their potentialities as human beings, a need which is not solely defined by their sexual role".(24)

Humanist Manifesto II, endorsed by Friedan,(25) states that our "ultimate goal should be the fulfilment of the potential for growth in each human personality", free of "traditional moral codes" and an "outmoded faith" in "a prayer-hearing God". The *Manifesto* demands "freedom of choice" and the right to birth control, abortion, divorce and all types of "sexual exploration".(26) Secular Humanism, allied with Marxism, atheism, agnosticism, rationalism and liberal religion,(27) became the intellectual fuel for the new feminism.

This feminism, now thoroughly Marxist, replaced the Christian concept of motherhood with the Communist ideal promoted by Friedan. Helping Friedan was child-care "expert" Dr Benjamin Spock, who postulated that Russian children, whose mothers worked, were emotionally more stable than American children "whose full-time mothers do nothing but worry about them".(28)

Later, disturbed by early marriages and the larger families being raised by housewives,(29) Friedan founded *NOW* (the *National Organisation for Women*), to lead the Humanist fight for "freedom of Choice" in moral matters, and for getting married women out of the home and into the work force,(21) with the object of reducing the birthrate. But Friedan's ideas were hardly original. Engels had already stated that the liberation of women demanded "as its main precondition . . . the reintegration of the whole female sex into the public industrial sector, with children being raised by the state".(30)

Recognising that feminism would be opposed by traditional religion, Friedan took the offensive, accusing ministers, priests and rabbis of "prejudice" because the "housewife image . . . is enshrined in the canons of their religion . . . and in their church's dogmatic definitions of marriage and motherhood".(31) The Catholic Church, as yet relatively free of feminism, was the chief opponent of its new family-wrecking mentality and it had to be destroyed.

Secular feminism could not do this from without. However it found a convenient tool in religious feminism, which also re-emerged in the 1950s, still mostly in Protestant denominations. The opportunity for attack arose in the late 1960s when the post-Vatican II experimentation in women's religious orders(32) provided the right soil for socialistic religious feminism to spread its roots into Catholicism. Nuns, angry at being "pushed around by the patriarchal structure", provided the attacking force.(33) Such a great number of nuns spearheaded the women's ordination movement that feminists themselves consider nuns the *"trendsetters for the modern women's liberation movement"*.(34) *(emphasis added)*.

Yet the Council itself cannot be blamed for the emergence of feminism in the Catholic Church. European Catholic women had been demanding ordination since the 1930s,(35) and the demands increased with the ordination of Swedish Lutheran women and the recognition of ordination as a civil right by mainstream Protestantism.(36) Large numbers of Catholic women who enrolled in non-Catholic theological colleges and seminaries following Vatican II(37) would have encountered these influences as well as the World Council of Churches' propaganda that the struggle against sexism is "an integral part of liberation theology" and the "Christian goal" should be "alliance with the Socialist cause, so that a world will be created from which, in accordance with *Galations 3:28*, all discrimination will be banished".(38)

Besides demanding ordination, religious feminists also aligned themselves with their secular sisters who had espoused the Marxist vision of womanhood that fuelled the secular liberation movement. Sharing their humanist goals, spiritual feminists started demanding "equality of opportunity" in the Church and autonomy in moral matters like contraception, abortion, divorce and lesbianism.(41) The Catholic Church's uncompromising stand on sexual morality only intensified their charges of "oppression".(42)

In Catholicism itself, the mistranslation and misinterpretations of conciliar and other Church documents that referred to women's changing place in society,(39) but upheld the Church's traditional teachings against a false notion of the equivalence of the sexes found in socialist ideology,(40) were used as "proof" that the Church approves of women's equality in theory, but not in practice. This justified the feminist revolution against the Church's "oppression".(42)

In the 1970s, "the return to the goddess" movement of the nineteenth century merged with Socialism in the new religious feminist movement. The decline into paganism of the majority of feminists started with the use of inclusive language. This brought about a rejection of God because of His "maleness", leading to the substitution of the "goddess within" for Him and the need to worship this deity, a need expressible only through witchcraft.(43) Calling themselves "Woman-Church", spiritual feminists re-wrote the Bible, invented "feminist theology" and adopted the rites of paganism and witchcraft for their "liturgies".(44)

St Francis Xavier Cabrini once pointed out that, since "nations are formed on the knees of the mother", then the more the mother is venerated and the more she conforms her conduct to Mary, who "raised the status of humanity", so much the greater will future generations and the nation be.(45) Feminists, co-operating willingly with the forces of evil that have denigrated Christian womanhood and motherhood, share the blame for the obvious decline of Christianity and Western civilisation.

The dangers of feminism were perceived as early as 1876 by Cardinal Gibbons of Baltimore. He put the crusade for "women's rights, so called", in the same category as "moral shams", "pious frauds" and "socialistic schemes which are so often undertaken . . . ostensibly in the name of religion and morality, but which . . . are subversive of morality and order, which are the offspring of fanaticism, and serve as a mask to hide the most debasing passions".(46)

The irony is that women who have striven hard for "liberation" from men have descended into *slavery* – the slavery of paganism from which Christ freed us – by being manipulated by wicked *men!* As noted above, those planning to conquer the world consider the corruption of women indispensable to their schemes; " . . . we can reform the world if we reform women".(8)

60

Ten:

The story of
Miss Teen Canada

Betty Steele

In Canada, a **Miss Teen Canada Pageant** and Television Special sponsored by CTV, the country's national commercial television network, was to become an astonishing historical landmark in events restoring dreams and hope to a people fast losing faith in their future.

It would seem that an ailing society had simply accepted a feminist dictatorship, rooted in socialist principles, with the entrenchment of feminist ideology in the *Canadian Constitutional Charter of Rights* of 1984 and had lost its strength or will, to combat all the appalling evils resulting from the women's liberation movement.

It has been acknowledged generally that feminist revolutionary leaders have accomplished more in Canada than in any other country in the western world. They have been responsible for legislating the incredible injustices against men in *Affirmative Action, Leap-frogging Laws* and the *Quota Systems*, culminating finally in 1989 in the Province of Ontario's *Pay Equity Law*. Abitrarily enforcing male and female job comparisons, with extreme punitive measures, it covers all private as well as public employers and has driven a significant number of men and businesses out of the province, while devastating family life-styles in those remaining. Premier David Peterson has boasted:

"Nowhere else in the world has such legislation been passed".

Nowhere else in the world has the very culture of a society been so radically and rapidly altered as in Canada, where many people have certainly been losing faith in the future of their country. With our birth rate the second fastest-falling in the world (after Japan), a government demographer predicted in 1989 that without massive immigration there would be no more Canadians by the year 2500. Massive immigration by 1990 meant that cities such as Toronto are already 67% ethnic and the English-French heritage obviously disappearing. In Quebec, with an even lower birth rate, the French language and culture is at greater risk, although the Quebec government is attempting to stem the tide with substantial tax advantages for mothers bearing the third and fourth child.

Blatant injustices in *Affirmative Action* were to be seen as feminist triumphs, when the Ontario College of Art, Canada's leading art school, announced in January 1990 that for ten years it would not accept any male applications for its teaching positions. In the same month the Ryerson Polytechnical Institute in Toronto, the leading school in its field in Canada, announced that it was only accepting female applications for its professorial positions that year.

Canada's precious children have been called "the throwaways" as women, persuaded by feminist ideology not to have children, resort to abortion as their careers are more important than babies; by postponing motherhood, a practice now known to be largely responsible for alarming infertility rates; and by government-funded feminist councils driving toward universal Stalinistic day-care. In 1985, there were studies showing 10,000 runaways on the streets of Toronto alone, with 12-year-old prostitutes being picked up by the police. By 1990, gangs of boys and gangs of girls were swarming in the big city shopping malls, terrorising shopkeepers and customers.

Suddenly onto such a distressing social picture, Canadians saw superimposed a wondrous phenomenon in the courage, character and strengths of 40 beautiful young cross-Canada finalists who came to Toronto for the *Seventeenth Annual Miss Teen Canada Pageant* and two-hour television special and dared to challenge feminist ideology.

The significance of the events of their week in Toronto would become evident, as we have always realised that our future and the future of the whole world, is ultimately in the hands of our children, our young people. In these young women we would discover that all our young people are not in trouble, and that they may indeed be stronger individuals for having survived the vicissitudes of a feminist revolution, with leadership qualities that could carry us all through the most difficult transitional period in our history.

"The Girls" were to become headline material, gaining the attention of Canadians from coast to cost, with their responses to a questionnaire in *The Toronto Star*, a national newspaper with the largest circulation in the country. The questions, were: "Do you consider yourself a feminist?" and "Do you have a role model?"

Basically, their reply to that first question was: "We are *not* feminists." They made such statements as:

We are who we are . . . We come from every Corner of Canada – our Canada of opportunities, opportunities that are not the gift of the women's liberation movement, as libbers would have us believe – but of our own way of life, our parents and our roots and governments . . .

We have our own ideas, our own beliefs, our own ambitions.

We intend to be in charge of our own lives, making our own successes, our own mistakes, our own future . . .

We will not be dictated to, or organised, or led by the nose into a way of life that we now see as highly undesirable.

As *The Toronto Star* columnists Lynda Hurst and Doris Anderson were the most militant feminists in the country, "The girls" might have expected the torrents of scorn and abuse in the ensuing newspaper's articles. The Girls were mercilessly belittled as "mindless" with their biggest problems "the appearance of a pimple, the disappearance of a date, or in this case, the winning of an inane beauty contest."

In a scathing response to one contestant, Lynda Hurst said: "Now I realise I'm not dealing with a doctoral scholar here . . ." In truth, she might have been dealing with a future doctoral scholar, as the intellectual abilities of the contestants were tested and proven above average.

From towns and cities across Canada, sponsored by their own communities and commercial enterprises, they had come to vie for the $100,000 in prizes and the honor and glamour of becoming *Miss Teen Canada, Miss Teen Fitness,* and *Miss Teen Friendship,* as well as competing in three special scholastic awards. While few of them, at an average age of 17, presumed they could win in any category, they had looked forward to having the experience of travelling to a big city, appearing on national television and of making new friends from other towns and provinces. According to the sponsors, making new friends was an invaluable and unifying element of the *Pageant.*

They were probably too young to remember what had happened in the *Miss Teen Canada Pageant* of 1975 which had been violently disrupted by feminists, resulting in one studio guard being hospitalised with broken ribs. In any case it is unlikely that The Girls would have been intimidated. In fact, they threw themselves further into the fray with another blistering retaliatory letter to their attackers on *The Toronto Star.* Eleven of them signed this letter:

> We do not appreciate your comments regarding that only a handful of us "appear to have grown up in the same world as the rest of us" . . . Feminist groups in this country support issues which many of us young and grownups of the future do not support. To us, feminists do not represent the women of today. They are a minority of vocal trouble-makers and therefore, our group wouldn't ever want to associate with them . . .

There were others, counter-attacking feminist political demands, who wrote,

> We do not believe in equal pay for equal value, but we believe in equal pay for equal work.

We do not think that Prime Minister Mulroney or our own provincial government leaders are unfair in not giving in to all those women's libbers who want a lot of things other Canadian women do not want . . . *but they do not.* They simply cannot force all Canadian women into one giant mold.

Teenagers against seasoned 40-60 year-old feminists and powerful publications such as *The Toronto Star* may have seemed an unequal battle, but in less than a month, there appeared an amazing revelation in all media . . . that the *Miss Teen Canada* contestants were probably speaking out for the majority of teen-age girls across the country.

President Sam Ion of the Ontario Advisory Council on Women's Issues reported on studies showing that "there are few feminists under the age of 35". In alarm, the federal Advisory Council on the Status of Women, with abundant federal funds always available, initiated another study of 150 adolescent girls from the ages of 15 to 19, covering five provinces. It revealed a marked absence of feminist goals. It also found that a majority of teen-age girls still had "rosy" dreams of being married, having loving husbands, trouble-free children, and home ownership; nor did they anticipate divorce in their lives.

These same aspirations and expectations were expressed in a survey of four hundred girls in grades nine through thirteen in six schools. Only 20% of the girls surveyed were interested in careers as lawyers, doctors or diplomats, while most of the others believed they would work happily in traditionally female occupations such as nursing, teaching or secretarial science, until they were married. Then they would assume the major responsibilities of homemaking and motherhood.

Doris Anderson in *The Toronto Star* asked in headlines: "Why should young girls live a fairy tale?" She insisted that many traditional jobs wouldn't exist within ten years because of technological advances (certainly a false premise). "Isn't it sad that girls can't be prepared to cope better with what's really ahead for them? Why do we put them through a living fairy tale again and again, before they are wakened up with a jolt?''

Mrs Anderson, a divorcee herself, pointed out that many of the girls have divorced parents and single mothers, and yet they would not face up to the fact that divorce could happen to them. The *Miss Teen Canada* contestants retorted heatedly, that it was not a foregone conclusion that it would happen to them! One of them wrote:

If that is the kind of world the old feminists would hand down to us . . . condemns us to divorce, single parenthood and lonely old age, well, then, are you surprised that we say NO, NO, NO, to feminism and try to reverse the trends? We think Women's Lib has produced many of those miserable conditions . . . driving a wedge between men and women.

When local newspapers across Canada, welcoming their contestants back home, asked for other teenagers' comments on the Toronto media battle, there was an overwhelming response. It seemed that *The Miss Teen Canada* contestants' courage had loosed all their tongues, inspiring them to express their own opinions. They repeated:

We girls want to be considered "persons" not segregated off into a corner of the ring as "Women's Libbers", who come out punching and clawing against the men at every imagined inequality . . . Men are not our enemies. We love our fathers, our brothers, our boyfriends and *we* still believe in *ordinary* happy marriages in spite of those divorce statistics . . . which we blame on the Women's Liberation Movement.

To *The Toronto Star's* question: "Do you have a role model?" the majority of *The Miss Teen Canada* contestants replied: "my mother", but other role models named over and over were Mother Teresa, and Mila Mulroney. Mila Mulroney, wife of the prime minister, had given up her engineering studies when she was seven months pregnant with their second child, and three subjects short of her degree. "A good marriage and motherhood are worth more than all the degrees you can get", she told one interviewer.

The girls across Canada stated flatly that there was not one feminist leader anywhere in the world they would choose as a role model. One 17-year-old wrote:

We sure wouldn't want Betty Friedan as a role model . . . We think a full-time home-mother has the most important job in the world. She 'makes' life and happiness for all members of her family, and often for all the relatives and community as well – my Mom does – she's even on the town council.

Seemingly, then, Canadian women of the future may no longer follow the feminist Pied Piper blindly into the workforce. Perhaps the bigger house, the fancy car, the restaurant meals, the extra holidays, the money for day-care, (later perhaps for divorce) which studies have indicated the second income provides . . . will never compensate for the exquisite joys and "self-fulfilment" of being a successful home-mother.

In their vision and courage, *The Miss Teen Canada* contestants gave us a whole new picture of society – in the return of a traditional family, with all its strengths, its moral commitments – the family that built up North America and has always been the very back-bone of our two nations on this continent.

We bless them for giving us back our faith in our future.

Appendix

Notes and References

Chapter 2: Feminism and the State – The Australian Experience *by Babette Francis*

1. Michael Levin, "Feminism and Thought Control", *Commentary*, June 1982.
2. *The Age*, Melbourne, November 9, 1985
3. Dinesh D'Souza, "Feminism's Counter-revolt", *The Washington Post*, January 26, 1986

Editor's note: This article is a slightly amended version of an original published in *Quadrant*, April 1987, and entitled "Feminism: the Six Frauds".

Chapter 6: A Radical Feminist Charter *by Valerie Riches*

1. U.N. Convention, Article 1
2. *Ibid.*, Article 5
3. *Ibid.*, Preamble para 9
4. *Ibid.*, Preamble para 14
5. *Ibid.*, Preamble para 12
6. *Ibid.*, Preamble para 7
7. *Ibid.*, Article 4:1
8. *Ibid.*, Article 11:2 d
9. *Quadrant*, November 1983
10. UN Convention, Article 11:2 c
11. *Ibid.*, Article 5 a
12. *Economic Eye*, June 1984
13. UN Convention, Article 10 c
14. *Ibid.*, Article 17:1
16. *The Human Right to Family Planning*, International Planned Parenthood Federation, 1984
17. A. Tuck, *The Australian Revolution*, Yandina, Q.4561

Chapter 7: Families, Feminism and Taxes *by Patricia Morgan*

1. Midge Dector, "For the Family", *Policy Review*, Winter 1984, No. 27, p.442
2. Mica Nava, "From Utopian to Scientific Feminism?" in Lynne Segal, *What is to be done about the Family*, Penguin Books in assoiciation with the Socialist Society, 1983, pp.66 and 69
3. C.C. Harris, *The Family and Industrial Society*, George Allen and Unwin, 1983, p.200
4. Melanie Henwood, *Inside the Family*, Family Policies Study Centre, 1987
5. See Peter Moss and Julia Brannen, "Fathers and Employment", in Charlie Lewis, *Reassessing Fatherhood*, Sage 1987, p.18
6. Melanie Henwood, *Op cit.*, p.18
7. Allan Bloom, *The unmaking of the American mind*, Simon Schuster, 1987, p.126
8. *Freedom and choice for Women*, Liberal SDP Alliance, 1986
9. C.C. Harris, *Op cit.*, p.216
10. "Child-care and Equality of Opportunity", Consolidated report to the European Commission, April 1988, p.27

71

11. David Piachaud, *Round about Fifty Hours a Week*, Child Poverty Action Group, 1984, p.22
12. "Child-care and Equality of Opportunity", *Op cit.*, p.28
13. Peter Moss and Julia Brannen, *Op cit.*, p.37
14. "Child-care and Equality of Opportunity", Consolidated report to the European Commission, *Op cit.*
15. *Ibid.*, p.21
16 Peter Moss and Julia Brannen, *Op cit.*, p.21
17. H. Graham, "Women's Poverty and Caring" in C. Glendinning and J. Millar, eds., *Women in Poverty in Britain*, Wheatsheaf, 1987, p.223
18. Bronwen Cohen, *Caring for Children: Services and Policies for Child-care and Equal Opportunities in the United Kingdom*, Commission of the European Communities, 1988, p.15
19. "Childcare and Equality of Opportunity", *Op cit.*, p.25
20. *Ibid.*, p.27
21. Peter Esam, Robert Good and Rick Middleton, *Who's to Benefit?*, New Left Books, 1985
22. See Penny Mansfield and Jean Collard, *The Beginning of the Rest of Your Life*, Macmillan, 1988 and Charles Lewis and Margaret O'Brien eds., *Reassessing Fatherhood*, Sage, 1987
23. Jean Martin and Ceridwen Roberts, *Women and Employment: A Lifetime Perspective*, Stationery Office, 1984
24. Roger Jowell, Sharon Witherspoon and Lindsay Brook eds., *British Social Attitudes: 4th report*, Social and Community Planning and Research, Gower, 1987
25. Lynne Segal, "The most important thing of all - Rethinking the Family: An Overview", in Lynne Segal, *Op cit.*
26. Catherine Itzin, *Splitting up: Single Parent Liberation*, Virago, 1980
27. Fran Bennett, "The State, Welfare and Women's Dependence", in Lynne Segal, *Op cit.*, p.200
28. *Ibid.*, p.201
29. *Ibid.*
30. *Family Wealth*, magazine, June 1987
31. *Sunday Times*, 10.2.85
32. "Freedom and Choice for Women", *Op cit.*

Chapter 8: The Female as Hamster by *Robert Whelan*

1. M.E. Spiro, *Gender and Culture: Kibbutz women revisited*, W.C. Durham, Duke University Press, 1979

Chapter 9: The Destructive Forces behind Religious Feminism by *Cornelia R Ferreira*

1. Rosemary Radford Ruether, "Radical Victorians: The Quest for an Alternative Culture", in *Women and Religion in America*, vol 3, 1900-1968, ed. Rosemary Ruether and Rosemary Skinner Keller, San Francisco, Harper and Row, 1986, pp.1-3
2. *Ibid.*, p.1
3. *Ibid.*, pp.1-3
4. *Ibid.*, pp.4-5
5. *Ibid.*, pp.2-4, Ruether cites as representative of their genre the 1861 work of the 'Swiss Classicist' Johan Bachofen, *Motherright*
6. *Ibid.*, p.4
7. *Ibid.*, pp.5, 1
8. Jose Maria Caro y Rodriguez, *The Mystery of Freemasonry Unveiled*, Santiago Society of the Good Press, n.d. 2nd ed., n.p., 1957, reprint ed., Hawthorn, CA, Christian Book Club of America, 1971, p.237

9. *Ibid.*, pp.237-238
10. Deidre Manifold, *Karl Marx*, Galway, Firinne Publications, 1985, p.72
11. Ruether, p.3, R. Ruether and R. Keller, "Introduction", *Women and Religion*, p.xiv
12. "Introduction" *Ibid.*
13. Ruether, p.3
14. Carol P. Christ and Judith Plaskow, "The Essential Challenge: Does Theology Speak to Women's Experience?" in *Womanspirit Rising: A feminist Reader in Religion*, ed. C Christ and J. Plakow, San Francisco, Harper and Row, 1979, p.19
15. Ruether, p.5
16. See footnote on Gal 3: 23-29, *The New American Bible*, Pope John Paul II edition, Nashville, Memorial Bibles International, 1977, p.1295
17. Rosemary Ruether and Eleanor McLaughlin, "Women's Leadership in the Jewish and Christian Traditions: Continuity and Change", in *Women of Spirit: Female Leadership in the Jewish and Christian Traditions*, ed., R. Ruether and E. McLaughlin, New York, Simon Schuster, 1979, p.25
18. Rev Manfred Hauke, *Women in the Priesthood*, trans. David Kipp, San Francisco, Ignatius Press, 1988, p.36
19. Ruether, "Radical Victorians", pp.2, 5, 9
20. *Ibid.*, p.9 and the explanation of her footnote 20, found on p.386
21. Alphonse de Valk, CSB, "Feminism's Basic Values", *The Interim*, Toronto, October 1985, p.16
22. *Ibid.*, also Hauke, *Ibid.*
23. Betty Friedan, *The Feminine Mystique*, New York, Dell Publishing Co. Inc., 1963, pp.8, 305-15
24. *Ibid.*, pp.351, 69
25. Paul Kurtz, ed., *Humanist Manifestoes I and II*, Buffalo, NY, Prometheus Books, 1973, p.28
26. *Ibid.*, pp.13-14, 18
27. *Ibid.*, p.15
28. For more on Spock-Friedan propaganda see Cornelia Ferreira, "The Emerging Feminist Religion", *Homiletic & Pastoral Review*, LXXXIX, No. 8, May 1989, p.12. Also published in pamphlet form, Toronto, Life Ethics Centre, 1989, see p.2
29. Friedan, pp.26, 42, 52-53, for example
30. Friedrick Engels, *The Origin of the Family, Private Property and the State*, 17th ed., Stuttgart, 1919, pp.62, 64, as cited in Hauke, p.31
31. Friedan, pp.338-39
32. Hauke, pp.61-62
33. Anne Roche Muggeridge, as quoted in E. Michael Jones, "What Lesbian Nuns can teach us about Vatican II", *Fidelity*, 5, No. 1, December 1985, pp.20-21; also see Jones, pp.17-19; cf. Hauke, pp.62-63
34. Barbara Haber, *Women in America, A Guide to Books*, 1963-75, Boston, 1978, p.155, as cited in Hauke, p.63
35. Ruether, *Sexism*, pp.217, 228-229; *idem.*, *Women-Church*, pp.192-195; and Lise Baroni, "The Creative Emergence of Women Working in the Church" in *Women for what World? In what Church?*, Ottawa, Canadian Religious Conference, 1985 p.50
36. Hauke, pp.44-45; Ruether and Keller, "Introduction", p.xix
37. Rosemary Radford Ruether, *Women-Church: Theology and practice of Feminist Liturgical Communities*, San Francisco, Harper and Row, 1985, p.65
38. Hauke, p.53
39. See Hauke, pp.55-60 for a detailed treatment of this subject. Texts particularly misconstrued are *Pacem in Terris*, 1963, 41, 43; The Dogmatic Constitution of the Church *Lumen Gentium*, 1964, 32; The pastoral Constitution of the Church in the Modern World *Gaudium et Spes*, 1965, 9; Decree on the Apostolate of Lay People *Apostolicam Actuositatem*, 1965, 9; and the Declaration on the Admission of Women to the Ministerial Priesthood *Inter Insigniores*, 1976, 5. Ignored for its upholding of the *differences* between the sexes is the Declaratation on Christian Education *Gravissimum Educationis*, 1965, 8. Cf. Muggeridge, p.21

40. Hauke, pp.55-57
41. See for instance, Ruether, *Sexism*, pp.217, 228-229; *idem.*, *Women-Church*, pp.192-195; and Lisa Baroni, "The Creative Emergence of Women Working in the Church", in *Women for what world? In what Church?*, Ottawa, Canadian Religious Coference, 1985, p.50
42. For example, see Diann Neu, SP, "Our Name is Church; the Experience of Catholic-Christian Feminist Liturgies", *Concilium*, No. 152, 1982, pp.75, 77, 81
43. Nelle Morton, "The Dilemma of Celebration" and Mary Daly, "After the Death of God the Father . . . " *Womanspirit*, pp.159-60, 56, 59; Patricia Wilson-Kastner, *Faith Feminism and Christ*, Philadelphia Fortress Press, 1983, pp.20-23
44. For a detailed description of this progression see Cornelia R. Ferreira, "The Feminist Agenda within the Church", *Homiletic & Pastoral Review*, LXXXVII, No. 8, May 1987, pp.14-16 or its pamphlet form, *The Feminist Agenda within the Catholic Church*, Toronto, Life Ethics Centre, 1987, pp.8-12; cf. Ruether and Keller, "Introduction", p.xiv
45. A Daughter of St Paul, *Mother Cabrini*, Boston, The Daughters of St Paul, 1977, p.54
46. James Cardinal Gibbons, *The Faith of our Fathers*, Baltimore, The John Murphy Company, 1876, repr., Rockford, Ill., Tan Books and Publishers, Inc., 1980, p.60